MW01690580

PRAISE FOR *BE THE ANSWER*

As I have traveled across the country, I have had the opportunity to meet many great leaders. Andrew Momon is one of those outstanding leaders who has always stood out to me, but for different reasons than most. Leaders are usually known because of their age or for the experience that they have gained over the years. Andrew, however, is young, yet still stands out because of his heart. Many leaders, unfortunately even Christian leaders, work so hard to be seen. Andrew stands out because he works so hard to serve. This is a totally different perspective of leadership. I love this book because it reflects the servant's heart that Jesus asks each of us to have. This book is challenging, it is thought-provoking, and it is a great read. I highly recommend it.

— Gerald Brooks, D.D., D.C.L.
Grace Outreach Center
Plano, TX

In these unusual, determining and challenging days, an answer-generation is arising that will push forth the Kingdom of God in this hour. Jesus teaches us, through His servant leadership in washing the feet of his disciples, that the *towel* is stronger than the sword! I know the life and ministry of Andrew Momon, and I am sure that through the principles in this book, which he has learned first hand, many people and ministries will become the answer of God for their generation. Congratulations, Andrew!

— Apostle Guido Raul Avila
Federation Christian Center for the Nations
Caracas, Venezuela

Jesus, the greatest example of a Servant Leader, is our example to follow, Paul writes for us in Philippians 2:9. Jesus, who being the very nature of God, made himself nothing and took on the very nature of a servant, humbled himself and became obedient to death. In dying God exalted Him to the highest place and gave him a name that is above every name. By dying to oneself and living to serve another, God examines the heart attitude and promotes one to his highest position.

Joshua served Moses, and Joshua was called by God as the next leader to lead and take the nation of Israel across Jordan. As a Prophet, Elisha served Elijah in faithfully serving; Elisha received a double portion of Elijah's anointing. Greatness is birthed from servanthood. There are only two jobs that start from the top, grave digging and well digging. All other jobs start from the bottom. *Be the Answer* is a great book to read, and it has a great wealth of knowledge. It's written with expert knowledge, and its application will promote you and position you for greatness, which is everyone's desire.

— Bishop DA Lazarus
Siloam Ministries
South Africa

Servant-Leadership. At first glance it seems like a paradox. A leader leads and a servant follows. However choosing between the two is asking which wing of the airplane is more important. They both are. In *Be the Answer* my friend Andrew Momon will share his transformative journey as a servant leader. Not only will his experience resonate with you, but you will also find pragmatic resources as you lead and serve better. You'll not just read this book yourself, but will want all your fellow servant-leaders to read it as well. Be ready to be transformed.

— Sam Chand
leadership consultant and author

BE THE ANSWER

Your guide to effective and transformative leadership

ANDREW MOMON JR

Be the Answer:
Your Guide to Effective and Transformative Leadership

by Andrew Momon, Jr.

copyright ©2015 by Andrew Momon, Jr.

published by Dream Releaser Publishing

Trade paperback ISBN: 978-1-943294-11-4
Ebook ISBN: 978-1-943294-12-1

Be the Answer is also available on Amazon Kindle, Barnes & Noble Nook and Apple iBooks.

Scriptures taken from The Message. Copyright © 1993, 1994, 1995, 1996, 2000, 2001, 2002. Used by permission of NavPress Publishing Group

CONTENTS

DEDICATION

I DEDICATE THIS BOOK TO ALL the unmentioned and unnamed individuals who know deep down inside they are an *answer* to the problems of this generation. To those who have for years and even decades been the ones behind the scenes making things happen for others so that a greater goal could be reached. I want to encourage you to never look at yourself as less than or of lesser importance simply because your name is not being called or you're not being recognized right now. Know that you are making a difference and that, without you, the leaders whose names are called and those who are being recognized publicly would not be able to do what they do as effectively. You are important to this world and *you are the answer to the problems of this world!* As I state in my acknowledgments, behind every problem there is a promise, and I encourage you to *be the answer* and receive the promises that are available to and for you!

ACKNOWLEDGMENTS

I WOULD LIKE TO ACKNOWLEDGE a few individuals that have been instrumental in my journey. When talking about "being the answer," there are a lot of phases you go through, asking and facing questions. These questions are life's interrogative measures that make us who we are. These individuals who have helped me on my journey have all been pivotal in me finding ways to develop the mindset of being an answer to problems. I have been taught in my upbringing that there is always a way to solve any problem that we're faced with. I have been taught to never quit, that the word "can't" does not apply to me, that I can do all things through Christ who gives me strength, that behind every problem there is a promise, that you have to push past all impediments and find *the answer* to the problem to take hold of all the promises meant for you.

I want to first thank my wife Dr. Kendra Momon who has been extremely instrumental in pushing and encouraging me to get this message of servant leadership out and share with others the journey I have been on—one that has spanned over half my life. If it weren't for you gently but persistently encouraging me to push through and finish this book, I can honestly say that I don't know if it would be in print today. Kendra, your love for me, the value of your commitment to me and your support to the call on my life is immeasurable. I am and will be forever grateful for who you are to me and how you love me! *I love you, Babe!*

Thanks to my parents who have instilled in me from an early age the mindset of service. From a child I was taught to do unto others as I would have them do unto me. You all brought different values to my life and planted seeds in me that now are harvesting and yielding great dividends, not only in my life, but now the lives of so many others who will read this book and utilize it as a resource to serve and add value to others.

To my brothers, Arron, Alexander, Trehvis and Dorian and my sister Kristin: thank you for allowing me to serve you over the years as your older brother. Being the oldest of all of my siblings, I learned at an early age the value of serving as a leader. You all have expressed at some point that you have looked up to me and the life that I have been graced to exemplify, and this is truly humbling. To be able to be a role model to members of my family truly means a lot to me. I love you all!

Lastly but not least, I give honor to my Pastor, Mentor, and Friend in Bishop Eddie L. Long. I thank you for seeing something in me before I saw it in myself. For helping develop the leader within me. For your example of serving others, even when based on your position and role, most would think that you expected to be served. What I have witnessed over the past 15 years of walking with you has been the total opposite. I have seen you serve those close to you, as well as this world, by giving of your time, talent and resources to see so many others blessed. You have been a great example of the teaching of Jesus that states, "The greatest among you must first be a servant." Thank you for investing in me so that I can now invest and be a blessing to others. I am forever grateful.

FOREWORD

A LITTLE OVER 14 YEARS AGO I met a very dedicated, enthusiastic, and honorable young man named Andrew L. Momon, Jr. While this was the first time I met him personally, he had been a member of the church for several years, serving alongside some of my sons in the ministry. So while I didn't know him personally, I knew of him and how he served—especially within our athletics summer camp. Interestingly, before I ever had direct knowledge or experience of it, Andrew was allowing God to position him to be the answer in the lives of others throughout New Birth.

Fast forward 14 years, and today Andrew is one of my key go-to players within the ministry, as well as the executive staff. No matter how large or small the task, I can call on Elder Momon, Andrew, or "Mo," as most everyone around the world affectionately calls him, gets the job done in excellence, without criticism or complaint. I am wholeheartedly convinced that God sent Andrew to uphold my arms and assist in bringing the vision and call on my life into full manifestation. And, over the past 14 years, he has done so even at great personal expense, to which I am forever grateful.

In *Be The Answer,* Andrew pens a compelling, captivating, and life transforming book that provides insight, direction, and wisdom to the "Jonathans" in a leader's life. To me, the "Jonathans" are the God-anointed and appointed, courageous, honorable, humble and loyal servant leaders who are willing—like Christ—to lay down their lives for their own. They are people sent by God to help leaders become all that God has ordained them to be. As 1 Samuel 14:6-7 reminds us, "Then Jonathan said to the young man who bore his armor, 'Come, let us go over to the garrison of these uncircumcised; it may be that the Lord will work for us. For nothing restrains the Lord from saving by many or by few.' So his armorbearer said to him, 'Do all that is in your heart. Go then; here I am with you, according to your heart.' "

As I always say of Andrew, "It takes a greater man to make a man great!" In *Be the Answer,* he helps leaders identify some of the critical characteristics necessary to identify *armorbearers* (those who carry you into purpose and destiny) while simultaneously protecting leaders from *pallbearers* (those who carry you to destruction and death)! Moreover, *Be the Answer* is designed to provide insight, direction and fortitude to those who know they have been called by God to bring vision and manifestation to fulfillment in the lives of others. In this regard, it is a *must-read* for leaders and servant leaders alike!

As one of Andrew's leaders and mentors, there are so many stories I can share about the 14-year journey God has entrusted to us. However, the key word in our journey is "trust"! I had to trust him to be the answer when I had a major meeting at my church, but the pilot said we couldn't land at our designated airfield. Andrew suggested that we land at another airfield. Praise the Lord, we made it to the event safely and on time. I had to trust him to be the answer when God mandated that we have an international conference with predominantly Spanish-speaking leaders and delegates, and he taught himself enough conversational Spanish to collaborate with the international team and our team to coordinate a very successful kingdom conference. And I have to trust him—even now—as God placed the mandate on his heart to write this book, for such as time as now, for all those who desire to and are called to be the answer.

I highly and enthusiastically encourage you to read this book from cover to cover and then go back and read it again. The gems God has deposited in this book through Andrew are absolutely astounding. I am in awe of God and of the ways in which he has allowed this true servant leader to exemplify and model the leadership principles of Jesus Christ both in this book and in his professional and personal life. Like the centurion soldier in the New Testament, Andrew understands true authority, and I am honored to have him be the answer as God continues to lead, guide and direct us through this kingdom journey.

— *Bishop Eddie L. Long*

INTRODUCTION

"On the way to stated leadership, first comes servant leadership." — Andrew Momon Jr.

SERVICE IS A WORD THAT for many conjures thoughts of inferiority. Thus, more often than not, individuals do not associate service or the act of serving others as a vital attribute of leadership. Be the Answer highlights some of the key attributes to being an effective leader and serves as a guide for cultivating leadership rooted in service.

Why is this important? America is starving for better leadership. The deficits, failures, and lack of progress in most facets of society, whether it's in government (politics), the church (the religious sector), or the educational system, is clear evidence that America is greatly in need of more effective leaders.

I'm certain there are many theories as to why we are failing to produce a greater number of effective leaders in various facets of American society. From my personal and professional perspective, there are three primary reasons for this deficiency. Firstly, leadership is a concept that frequently is misused and improperly defined. More often than not, the concept of "serving others" is not easily associated with the inherent attributes of leadership. Yet, when closely examining the true definition of leadership, in the words of Robert Greenleaf, "Leadership begins with a natural feeling that one wants to serve." In other words, true leadership is rooted in finding the greatest sense of fulfillment in serving others. Thus, the inspiration for being a leader and the ultimate goal of leadership should not be for personal accolades or to be placed on a pedestal. Rather, it should be to serve.

Secondly, there is a lack of mentorship being provided when it comes to true and authentic models of servant leadership. This can be because few of us are fortunate enough to have in our daily presence an individual who exhibits leadership that is focused more on others than themselves. Individuals, then, are faced with the challenge of not only learning a more accurate and healthy definition of leadership but of attempting to embody a high standard of leadership without a readily available support system to reinforce their values. Thirdly, and just as significant, we're breeding a culture of young people who prematurely want the authority and accolades that come with being a leader before first fully committing themselves to serving others.

Immediate gratification has become a predominant value of our culture. Living in an age where more and more people are preoccupied with how many digital followers they have, the art of being an unsung hero is rapidly declining as it becomes less common to find individuals who don't need their name to be called in order for them to be effective.

This is further compounded by the fact that many youth and young adults do not have access to a clear process of training to become effective leaders let alone to become servant leaders. Or, when a clear process or rites of passage is in place, they devalue the process and attempt to bypass or circumvent the critical stages of leadership development that require one to first learn how to serve others before being entrusted with greater levels of responsibility and authority over others.

Servant leaders are not created overnight. Instead, servant leadership has various stages of growth and development involving an ongoing cycle of refining and sharpening one's skills and belief system. These stages are a prerequisite to learning to be an effective leader. *Be the Answer* provides readers with a philosophy and principles for cultivating leadership as well as a path and clear stages for developing themselves in order to be in a position to help complete others. What do I mean by "to complete others?" "Completing others," simply put, is approaching service to others and one's role within an organization with a positive attitude and the goal of providing the missing skills and insight to help the leader achieve his or her overall vision for the organization or company.

Be the Answer, in addition to presenting a broader definition of leadership that directly correlates with service to others, highlights the "Five Attributes of an Effective Servant Leader." In doing so, it offers real-life scenarios of how other principles of leadership can be effectively applied and guides the reader through the self-exploration and self-examination required to transform oneself into an effective servant leader.

As previously stated, mentorship is a key component in the process of developing servant leaders. This has proven to be true in my personal journey. A number of positive experiences in my youth initially shaped and laid a foundation for my understanding of servant leadership. More recently, over the past 14 years, I have been blessed with the privilege and the honor of serving an awesome

CEO, entrepreneur, philanthropist, family man, and man of God: Bishop Eddie L. Long, Sr. Pastor of New Birth Missionary Baptist Church in Lithonia, Georgia. In my role as his personal assistant, I have met heads of states, diplomats, corporate giants, great men and women of faith, athletes, entertainers, and the like. Given the heart and vision of this awesome man of God, I have also been in front of thousands of unknown and "nameless" everyday people who also have significance in their respective spheres of influence.

In addition to these amazing experiences, as a lifelong learner, I have also sharpened and fine-tuned my philosophy on servant leadership by reading and studying materials on the subject matter from experts such as Robert Greenleaf, who is recognized as the founder of the concept and foremost authority on servant leadership. My continual growth and development as a leader has also been significantly aided by having the opportunity to leverage my initial role as a Personal Assistant into new roles of greater responsibility, authority, and influence. Expanding beyond my role as an employee of the church, I have also begun to share my knowledge and understanding of leadership development and service to others as the co-founder of a consulting firm with my wife Dr. Kendra Momon (*momonleadership.com*) and facilitator of workshops and seminars.

These life experiences have culminated in my current mission in life, which is to help train the next generation of servant leaders. This book is a tool to fulfill this mission; it is designed to help individuals at all levels of leadership. Whether it's being a baseball coach or being a supervisor at your job, learn some of the important qualities of leadership and how to develop and implement them into one's personal and professional life. Thus, there are no limitations on the type of religious, business, or organizational settings in which the leadership principles presented in this book can be applied.

Much of the message in this book is that there is honor in being second. Meaning, even though you may not be the person upfront in a leadership role, you're still extremely vital. This is a very important and valuable message, given the role of seconds often goes under-appreciated and unnoticed. Yet, the manifestation of the leader's vision would not be possible without the right team and supporting cast, people willing to surrender their egos to a higher purpose, mission, and calling. The expertise, insight, and people skills of support staffers fill many of the missing gaps in leadership of the first in command while simultaneously offering invaluable support and a greatly needed sense of trust to those primary leaders.

The manifestation of the leader's vision would not be possible without the right team and supporting cast, people willing to surrender their egos to a higher purpose, mission, and calling.

With that being said, the message of this book has specific relevance for those whose current aspiration is to one day become the primary leader of their company or organization. The reality is that not everyone can become the primary leader, but everyone does have an important role to play in the success of their organization or any team they're part of. This is why it is critically important for me to emphasize that we all are called to serve in one form or another because we all are placed on this earth with a unique life purpose. It's up to us to commit ourselves to finding what that is and feeling a sense of joy and fulfillment in doing it. We, however, can only do this by first fully embracing the concept of servant leadership and by truly believing that "the greatest among us are servants"—that one of the greatest things anyone can do is to live a life of service unto others. In essence, this means embracing the role of being a servant with a positive attitude and by always giving 200 percent in whatever role we find ourselves. In every moment, give your all. Show up every day ready to serve—focused on withholding nothing.

Chapter 1

THE PSYCHOLOGY OF A SERVANT LEADER

"Some things cannot be taught, they have to be caught."
— Bishop Eddie L. Long

SERVANT LEADERSHIP REQUIRES a certain mindset. More than anything, it requires a surrendering of one's ego for the greater good. Being of service requires one to first think about the needs of others, which can be very challenging to do—especially today in a society that tends to lean more toward a self-preserving and self-serving outlook on life. Many individuals want the glory or to at least be recognized for their good works. But, when one fully commits to serving others, there are no guarantees or assurances that one will ever be fully recognized for his or her contributions.

A certain kind of psychology is required to be a highly effective servant leader. What do I mean by psychology? You may be saying to yourself while reading this book, "It can't be that hard can it?" Are you saying, "There's more to servant leadership than just being a good person and wanting to volunteer or help someone else? Or, is it serving a cause and higher purpose until I can get to a place where I become the leader?"

What I mean is that one has adopted a certain way of thinking, being, and processing life events and the priorities in one's daily work activities. One has removed any barriers that may hinder him or her from being in tune and responsive to the needs of their primary leader and others to whom they may provide a service.

This is particularly relevant for men. We are often born with a certain amount of baggage dumped on us by society as to what it means to be a man and serving others. More often than not, men are encouraged to embody the persona of a gladiator or someone who at all costs stands in the forefront, figuratively or symbolically, beating his chest making a show of strength and independence. Subsequently, a man with this thinking can be at a deficit or resistant to the idea of fully investing himself in the concept of servant leadership or of being a servant to anything, let alone to another person. The core value of humility may have become distorted in his thinking. Instead, the concept of servant leadership must be promoted to capture the real essence that is intended in its true meaning. Resistance to the concept and philosophy of servant leadership can ring true for women as well. Many women today detest the idea of being subservient to anyone. Women with this mindset will resist any role offered or suggested to them in which the primary function is to support and "serve" the needs

> Service, in and of itself, is part of the natural order of life. It is the way God intended things to be.

of another person. Yet, when you really think about it, on some level or to some degree, we all serve others in our daily lives. As parents, we serve our children. As employees, we serve our bosses. So, service, in and of itself, is part of the natural order of life. It is the way God intended things to be.

> Let nothing be done through selfish ambition or conceit, but in lowliness of mind let each esteem others better than himself. Let each of you look out not only for his own interests, but also for the interests of others (Philippians 2:3).

Everyone can serve and everyone is called to serve in some form or fashion! The question is whether or not you will fully surrender to that calling, or will you allow the fear of how you will be perceived by others block you or interfere with you fully living out your purpose?

Part of my goal with this book is to challenge you to be all that you were created to be. I believe learning and developing a mindset of servant leadership is crucial to doing so. Otherwise, you'll live a life of perpetual concern about your status and how you're perceived by others. This is precisely why so many people are not where they are supposed to be in life or have not met their potential. They succumb to adult peer pressure instead of fully exercising their gifts, talents, God-given abilities, and calling in life.

Overall, this book can help the reader move toward fulfilling his or her potential in a number of areas in their life. I, however, within the context of writing this book, would like to devote much of my attention to individuals whose primary work or volunteer responsibilities consist of being directly in service to others and more specifically to primary leaders. This would include individuals who are Personal Assistants/Church Armor Bearers (Secretaries, Administrative Assistants), Executive Staff, and any other role where you're not the primary leader or the man or woman out front, but you have the opportunity to positively affect change in your organization by how well you provide service upline.

It's equally important to note, that while much of the principles and philosophies discussed in this book are rooted in Biblical principles, these same principles and philosophies can be applied to individuals working in a wide range of settings (church/religious, corporate, volunteer, community organizations, etc.).

So, how does an individual go about developing the right psychology for being an effective servant leader?

- Understand the importance or significance of why one should serve.
- Ask yourself if you view service or being a servant as a sign of weakness?
- Ask yourself, "Am I doing all that I can do to be of service to others?"
- Begin practicing, on a daily basis, serving others to the best of your ability.

1. UNDERSTAND THE IMPORTANCE OR SIGNIFICANCE OF "WHY" ONE SHOULD SERVE.

In the next chapter, which is entitled "The Need and Value of Servant Leaders," we'll go into greater detail regarding the topic of "why" one should serve. However, for now, it's important that we briefly discuss this topic given its close relation to the psychology of being a servant leader

People understand the importance of their service when they see the God-given big picture or the organization's ultimate goal being accomplished. A lot of times that big picture is not accomplished because people lose sight of the long-term goal. They want to focus more on themselves than on the role they play in the bigger scheme of things. What should be paramount is that the project is finished and the overall positive impact that it's going to have on others.

What happens is that, sometimes we don't want to be a part of the unsung or the unrecognized. We want our name to be called all the time even though that's impossible. Everyone is not going to be the main man or woman who is in the limelight as the primary leader. Some people have to be the workers, the team that supports the primary leader.

A true servant leader understands and accepts this reality (the "why" behind what they're doing). Because their psychology is one that is programmed to focus more on the team than on "I," they're a person whose name doesn't need to be called. They are okay with simply being a part of the multitude. What drives and fulfills them is making sure the project happens. Their end goal is ensuring that the task is complete and that they were the answer to any problems that arose in the process of completing the task and fulfilling the ultimate goal or mission.

2. ASK YOURSELF IF YOU VIEW SERVICE OR BEING A SERVANT AS A SIGN OF WEAKNESS?

As stated earlier, many of us are conditioned to give service or being a servant a negative connotation. There are, however, many examples to pull from in learning to see service and being a servant in a more positive light. In the Bible, numerous scriptures and stories illustrate the power of service. One of them is:

"The greatest among you must be a servant."
— Matthew 23:11 (NLT)

Servanthood is not based on someone's weakness; it's actually showing strength and humility. I once even heard someone say, "Humility is simply strength under control." Today, I frequently find that humility is mostly interpreted as weak and lowly, when at its foundation, it is very much the opposite. Humility requires a certain degree or level of strength to know when and how to exemplify self-control to accomplish the needed objective. So, to make the shift in your psychology, you first have to see yourself as strong and valuable regardless of your designated role. If you do identify barriers with regards to how you perceive your role as a servant leader, these are some helpful steps you can begin to take:

Servanthood is not based on someone's weakness; it's actually showing strength and humility. Humility is simply strength under control.

a. Begin journaling to work through creating a healthier definition of service for yourself to become fully comfortable with serving others.

There are subconscious variables at play in the everyday actions of every individual. Your goal is to become aware of any barriers to being an effective servant leader and work to remove them. Journaling or keeping a diary is an excellent tool for facilitating this process. An individual, for example, may be walking around and acting out their emotions in a passive-aggressive manner. There may be underlying emotions and resentment with thoughts and feelings of "When is it my time?" or "What about me?" If you're willing to be honest about how you're feeling and willing to confront your emotions head-on, then you can begin retraining your mind and actions to be in alignment with the principles and attributes of servant leadership.

b. Identify tangible role models of servant leadership you can talk to or look to for guidance.

Another invaluable tool for strengthening your perception and understanding of what it means to be an effective servant leader can be found in a tangible role model. It's very likely that they've already been down the same road you are headed down and have overcome some similar challenges. Even if the perspective that they have to offer is that of a leader, manager, and supervisor of teams, there is much to be learned. We all have blind spots and sometimes those are fueled by our emotions. So, if nothing else, a good mentor will be able to help you express your emotions in a safe environment while simultaneously challenging you to continue to grow, evolve, and expand from your current point of view. I received the benefit of a mentor in the realm of servant leadership when I first started in my role as a personal assistant, and it has yielded immense dividends.

c. Read books and/or attend trainings on servant leadership.

When a tangible mentor is not available, that's no excuse for not continuing to grow and challenge yourself. Particularly with the ever-growing data available through the Internet, an individual can access online information about just about any topic imaginable. When a tangible mentor is present, reading books and attending training can be an added bonus. They can reinforce what is being learned and absorbed from being around your mentor.

If you don't have a tangible mentor yet, you can utilize this book as a form of mentorship. I provide resources throughout this book as well as on my website (www.momonleadership.com).

3. ASK YOURSELF: "AM I DOING ALL THAT I CAN DO TO BE OF SERVICE TO OTHERS? IN MY HEART, IS THERE MORE THAT I KNOW I SHOULD BE DOING TO SERVE OTHERS?"

"To thy own self be true."
— William Shakespeare

True fulfillment of the function of giving your all in service can only truly be known by you. All of us know when we could do more. The problem occurs when we mislead ourselves. Hence, at times, self-interrogation is the biggest and most important form of measurement. This keeps you from having to be corrected and allows you to make behavioral turns without having to learn the hard way.

One of the keys to true servant leadership is that it has to be done from the heart and not because you want to be recognized for it. For me personally, my approach to serving is that I am doing it as an act of worship unto God, not to man. I do it as if God is inspecting my work, which I believe and know he is.

4. BEGIN PRACTICING, ON A DAILY BASIS, SERVING OTHERS TO THE BEST OF YOUR ABILITY.

A true servant leader is excited about being a "completer." Without hesitation or reservations, they take pride and joy in their role of supporting their leader and willingly make the necessary sacrifices that come with the job. For such individuals, the role of serving others feels like a natural extension of themselves. For others, learning to embrace the psychology of being a servant leader takes time.

In such instances, when one has not yet fully embraced the concept and psychology of being a servant leader, it's even more paramount that the individual at minimum is willing to make a commitment to practicing. This can at least provide a starting point. More than anything, a person's heart needs to be in the right place. That's where it all begins—in an individual's heart, with his or her sense of compassion and understanding of the importance of service.

That's where it all begins—in an individual's heart, with his or her sense of compassion and understanding of the importance of service.

Begin with finding a heart that is genuinely passionate about serving others. Find and even create opportunities to sow service into others. I'm a firm believer in the biblical principle "What a man sows he will also reap." Inevitably your psychology will change. Over time, with practice, you can and will become a highly effective servant leader because this principle doesn't lie. You will see as you practice it that you will begin to reap the benefits of your service to others. A major benefit that will become clearly evident is that you will begin to get joy out of seeing others get answers to even the simplest of problems they face. Look for this as a clear sign and indication that you are on your way now to becoming *the answer.*

TAKEAWAYS

- One can develop the psychology of being a servant leader.
- Self-evaluation and self-interrogation are essential steps in this process.

- Everyone has the opportunity to be a servant.
- Don't serve seeking the approval of man. (Intentions are very important).

Chapter 2

THE NEED FOR AND VALUE OF SERVANT LEADERS

ALL GREAT COMPANIES, ORGANIZATIONS, AND movements require a team, a highly functioning team. Teams are comprised of individuals and every individual has their own unique role. Some are leaders. Some are managers. Some are solely devoted to supporting the needs of leaders and managers. These individuals I refer to as the "ground crew."

I borrow the ground crew concept from the work and life of Dr. Martin Luther King, Jr. In his autobiography, Dr. King acknowledged that although he was the recipient of the Nobel Peace Prize, the prize was actually won by all the *noble* people who participated in the great civil rights struggle of America. When Dr. King was asked, "How did it feel to receive such a high honor?" he said that he was at a loss for words until he remembered a rare moment of silence in his study. That's when the clear correlation of how a flight's ground crew can be compared to the team members of the civil rights movement came to him.

He continued by sharing the story of being on a flight (preparing to take off), looking down, and seeing all these men working diligently to ensure that the flight would be free of mechanical difficulty to make it safely to its destination. The men who served were called the "ground crew." Although the pilot and flight attendants were well able and capable, if it had not been for the ground crew, the flight could not have taken off.

Dr. King shared the credit of winning the Nobel Peace Prize with the ground crew, because during the civil rights movement, fifty thousand Negroes in Montgomery, Alabama gave up their seats for 381 consecutive days. It was their commitment, struggle, and sacrifice that helped the bus boycott take flight and reach international acclaim. Dr. King may have been the pilot, but without a ground crew, none of it would have been possible.

This is a great example of the need for a ground crew. The pilot can try to fly the plane all he wants. But, when you start breaking down what all is entailed in getting a plane to fly, you soon realize that there are countless moving parts involved in the process. Someone has to fuel the plane. Someone has to perform maintenance on the plane. Someone has to handle air traffic control to make sure the plane's flight pattern doesn't interfere with other flights. If they get wrong information, or wrong instructions, they'll be off track and risk getting lost or even worse, having a collision. So, without the ground crew, without people who make the preparations for people to get on the plane and to reach their destination safely, none of it would be possible. While the pilot is highly valuable and ultimately in control of the aircraft, it clearly takes a team effort to fulfill the mission.

Dr. King's story offers a great example of how the natural tendency for most people is to focus their attention on the pilot, the person who's flying the plane or appears to be the leader, as the central person. Books, documentaries, and the like frequently highlight the accomplishments and greatness of Dr. King. However, without the ground crew, Dr. King would not have been able to attain the level of effectiveness and impact he attained. The same is true of a pilot. Without a ground crew, the overall goal of an airline getting people from Point A to Point B couldn't be accomplished. And, in this instance with Dr. King, without thousands of citizens willing to strike in the Montgomery Bus Boycott, the civil rights movement may have never gained longstanding momentum nationally. In light of this, according to Dr. King, these unknown soldiers did more than they will ever be acknowledged for. Even still, because of the team's commitment to servant leadership, they did not count it robbery to be of service to a cause bigger than themselves.

This is why Dr. King is one of my heroes and mentors. He epitomizes and symbolizes servant leadership and teamwork. As part of his philosophy and life principles, he didn't count it robbery to do two things:

1. Sacrifice personal time with the ones he loved the most (his family).
2. Acknowledge all the unknown soldiers who made it possible to do what he did (the ground crew).

THE ABILITY TO WORK IN THE CONTEXT OF TEAMS

The importance and value of teams should be stressed just as much as the need for servant leaders. They go hand-in-hand. Teams are needed, because no one individual can perform all roles. A team of servant leaders are needed because leaders or visionaries have many things placed on their plate and often have areas of weakness or blind spots that need to be filled in by support staff. Hence, there is a tremendous need and value for servant leaders and those willing to commit to fulfilling the vision.

Many leaders are gifted and have great visions to be fulfilled, but they aren't or won't be fulfilled unless they have a great team around them and an exceptional servant leader or leaders working directly under them. It's the role of the primary leader to speak the vision. It's the role of those around him to make it happen!

Primary leaders don't have time, nor should they be concerned with what we are doing in the background to present the final product of what they have charged us to do. It's the ground crew's responsibility to free up the leader to dream and be the visionary leader they are. The team does what it does so the primary leader is able to focus on executing his function, which is to lead.

Many leaders are gifted and have great visions to be fulfilled, but they aren't or won't be fulfilled unless they have a great team around them

What I believe inhibits so many individuals in supporting roles is that they often get caught up in wanting their names called or for them to be considered "the man." They want to be the leader, to be the person who's up front, so badly that they forget that their current role truly has tremendous importance and impact.

Bishop Long and I have a statement that we say to each other often when encouraging one another along our journey of working together. It's the familiar quote that says, "It takes a greater man to make a man great." This statement is so familiar and simple but so valuable and filled with truth. What it really comes down to is who the primary leader has behind them to make sure their organization thrives. It takes people who are committed to the advancement of that leader and what they have to offer the world. It takes a team!

Leaders need people around them who are able to work in teams and who enjoy being an *answer* to a problem. There are lots of leaders out there who are doing great things, but I would bet all my money that every person you see up front has an awesome team behind them, making sure things are happening. Leaders must have people around them who can transfer what they see and feel into tangible steps that can be executed toward fulfilling the vision.

In my ministry functions at New Birth Church, I have the privilege of working with a great team. A key lesson that I've learned from being out on ministry assignments is that it takes an entire team to ensure all sides of our assignment to Bishop Long and his vision are completed. Some of us handle the administrative pieces, some handle pre-assignment logistics, and others hold it down at our home while we're out to ensure that the standard of excellence is held up. With this in mind, I'd like to take a moment to acknowledge a few of the members of the ground crew on our team:

Leaders must have people around them who can transfer what they see and feel into tangible steps that can be executed toward fulfilling the vision.

April McLaughlin

Diana Williams

Lori Allen

Roberto Woods

Horatious Harris

Carla Stokes

Maurice Waddell

Dr. King's analogy of the ground crew still has tremendous relevance today. In every arena of life, there are modern day ground crews. When presented with the analogy of a ground crew, servant leaders can easily conceptualize how the work they do is essential. It emphasizes that no task is too small. This is significant given that we live in a day and age where everyone wants to be seen and heard. Thus, being a part of the ground crew allows your life work and actions to speak for you. It allows your impact to be felt versus seen. Being a part of the ground crew allows you to empower all who come in contact with you as you now have the opportunity to be a living example of servant leadership.

Each member of the ground crew must take ownership of their portion in the assignment and execute it with excellence. We have to have trust in one another and have confidence that others will do their parts. We also have to appreciate the gifting of each person's role and not diminish any component. There can be no big I's and little u's. It is important for every component to be in place for an airline to go smoothly. It takes every person performing their role to ensure the goal is accomplished.

Dr. King, also, in discussing the concept and analogy of a ground crew, identified some specific characteristics that participants in the Montgomery Bus Boycott in particular—and excellent ground crew members in any scenario—display:

1. Discipline
2. Wise restraint
3. Majestic courage

I, from my personal experiences, have also identified two additional characteristics of ground crew members that I think are very important to include in this list.

4. Selflessness
5. Foresight

When I look at these five qualities together, I look at them as symbolic fingers that when focused and combined toward a particular action are presented as a strong fist that can punch through any barrier that presents itself to hinder progress toward the goal. Ground crew members must be disciplined, have majestic courage, and exhibit wise restraint. As servant leaders, and equally as members of teams, we should strive to embody the characteristics of discipline, wise restraint, and majestic courage. We also must exhibit selflessness and foresight as these two additional characteristics make it possible for the necessary actions to be accomplished in properly supporting your leader or organization. When we are selfless and truly focused on the vision and goal of our leader, we will be compelled to do what is best for the team. We will see what needs to be done and take the initiative to do it without seeking fame or glory. We will relish and find fulfillment in our role as an *answer* and *completer*.

TAKEAWAYS

- All great leaders have a great supporting cast.
- The five qualities of a ground crew are: discipline; wise restraint; majestic courage; selflessness; and foresight.
- Do your part so your leader can do his part.

Chapter 3

A YES MAN OR A POINT MAN

In Chapter 1, "The Psychology of a Servant Leader," we spent a lot of time talking about having the right mindset. Part of that mindset has to do with how easily one is affected by how others perceive them in their role as servant leader. It's easy to fall into the trap of allowing other people to define who you are as a servant leader. Hence, I want to make a particular point in this chapter to caution against it.

Be prepared. People are going to—or already have—called you many names and titles to belittle you and your role. You, for example, may hear someone refer to you as: just an overpaid secretary, an errand boy or girl, a flunky, or even a slave. You have to have enough clarity, conviction, and contentment within yourself to not let such statements have a negative impact on you. Even more, you have to see the role of being a servant leader as one of power rather than weakness. Each day you wake up, you have to make the conscious choice to give of yourself in service to others, and that requires strength, courage, and discipline.

This internal sense of clarity is needed if you're going to fully carry out your duties and perform your role to the best of your ability. You can't be confused about what it means to be a servant leader. You have to have absolute certainty, and that's what I'm trying to offer you in this book. I want to drill home a definition of servant leadership that is rooted in strength and not weakness. I'm painting as clear a picture as possible of how essential and pivotal your role is to the overall success of an organization, company, and your leader's vision.

Visualize this. You're the point guard of the basketball team and this comes with great responsibility. Once the ball is put into play, you must dribble the ball up the court and help the team try to score a basket. That doesn't mean you're the star of the team. That doesn't mean you're the coach of the team. That doesn't mean you're the owner of the team. It means you're the point man!

Every team must have a point man, and that's your role. You need to know the role and function of every other member of the team like the back of your hand and make sure that they are in position to try to score a basket. If they're not, you need to direct them to a different location on the floor.

As the point guard of the team, that's exactly what you do. It's your job to manage the floor, to see where all the players are supposed to be. You can call plays. You can change plays if you see the plays you're running aren't working effectively and are putting your team in jeopardy of losing the game.

So, to me, all of this signifies strength. It signifies initiative. It signifies leadership, and that's exactly what primary leaders need. They DO NOT need a yes man or a yes woman. They need someone who can offer challenging insight and can take control of situations in their absence. They need someone who can problem-solve and find ways to be the answer.

The power of being a point man is that people can trust you. You are an effective communicator. They listen to you because they know you will tell them the truth in love even if it hurts you to do so. Ultimately, they grow to depend on you.

You carry your power and significance in a quiet manner. You are not concerned with accolades because your priority is getting the job done. You pride yourself on becoming the invisible man—meaning your impact is felt even if you are not seen.

Inherently, there are temptations and dangers to becoming a yes man even when you have been empowered by the primary leader to basically be the designated leader in his or her absence. Some individuals were raised in an environment in which they were socialized to never fully voice their opinions to authority figures. Their interpretation of this then is that they should be overly cautious. Thus, it produces a certain degree of fear of not wanting to rock the boat, overstep boundaries, offend, etc. Unfortunately, if you continue to carry this limited thinking, you cannot be fully effective in your job as that designated or support leader nor can you reach your full potential as a leader. Even worse, by not finding the right balance between exercising timely decision-making and knowing when to defer to se-

Great leaders do not need a yes man or a yes woman. They need someone who can offer challenging insight and can take control of situations in their absence.

nior figures, you run a greater risk of becoming a liability to those you serve rather than a completer.

Take me, for example, in my role as Bishop Long's Chief Assistant; there are many things that he says he wants to do. I could always just say "yes" to avoid conflict, or I could be honest when I don't think something is a good idea. The reason for this could be something as simple as the timing not being right. From my experience, I've learned that to truly serve your leader, you have to be able to speak up and say things without fear of being rejected. That's what your role is: to help the leader effectively and efficiently achieve his goals and the overall vision.

A perfect example of this happens when I'm driving my wife around town. We're enjoying our day engulfed in great conversation or just relaxing while we ride, when all of a sudden another vehicle does something erratic. As my wing person or point man in that situation, she has two options she can exercise in that moment. She can sit and assume that I saw the vehicle and hope that I avoid it, or she can say something quickly to ensure that I see it in enough time to avoid a possible accident. The factors impacting her decision to say something or not could vary, but I'll just bring light to a few.

One of the factors may be that my wife knows that sometimes when she shouts things like "look out" or "slow down," I get annoyed, because I feel as if I have it under control. I may say something like, "Babe, I see it" as a way of saying, "Let me drive." The flip side is that there *are* times when I don't see things, and the truth of the matter is I would rather she say something than let me run into a bad situation.

Because of our previous experiences in these types of situations, she has had to learn to measure when it's important for her to bring something to my attention or when it's best to let me handle it. Of course, when she speaks up, she runs the risk of possibly feeling a slight bit of rejection when I express that I have it under control. However, the pros far outweigh the cons in this situation because in speaking up, she keeps both of us alive. Even though I may not have wanted her to be a "passenger seat driver," I have learned to appreciate the value of her as a "point man" who is looking out for both of our interests. So, if I haven't told my wife Kendra how much I appreciate the times that she has spoken up when I needed to hear it, I want to do so now. Thank you, Kendra!

Accept the fact that your leader is always going to come up with ideas and want to try new things. That's the nature of a visionary.

Accept the fact that your leader is always going to come up with ideas and want to try new things. That's the nature of a visionary. Part of your job is to be a sounding board and to help them see major and minor details that they may be overlooking. They will appreciate and respect you for saying something versus sitting and letting them crash and burn.

Because I view a servant leader's role from this perspective, it's my belief that it's not always the leader's fault when problems happen in an organization. Those who serve in support roles have to and should shoulder some of the responsibility. A servant leader has to be able to see the blind spots. If the leader still decides or insists on going forward with a certain plan or moving in a certain direction, you at least will have given them the tools to know the pros and cons from the onset.

Leaders have to have people around them who are able to see things that they don't see (instead of just being along for the ride). And, as a servant leader, you have to become comfortable with saying, "Sir, I noticed the intent of what you want to do, but have you considered this?" versus just always saying, "Yeah man that sounds good. Let's do it" when you know you have reservations (or legitimate reasons for being concerned).

You can practice and find ways to tell him in honesty but in respect: "Sir I don't think that's a good idea. I don't think that you should go down that road because these are the things that will come from that."

It's not that you're trying to be the leader or tell them what to do, but your leader should have people with them who are competent and thus able to see and articulate things that they don't see or at least be able to bring observations to light. This requires actually speaking up without fear of being displaced, without fear of being fired, without fear of losing favor in their leader's eyes. This ability to speak up in crucial moments may not be validated immediately. You may have to practice with small things to build the trust with your leader. You do this so that a rapport of comfort is built over time, so that your leader sees that you ultimately have their best interests in mind. It may take you and your leader having real honest conversations as debriefing moments after situations so that you both gain an understanding of each person's perspective, which will build trust for future situations.

If the leaders still decide to do something that you've advised against, you can rest knowing that, at least you've spoken up, played your role, and given them the tools and outlook of what could potentially happen. Otherwise, you'll be saying to yourself, "I wish I would have said something." It's like I referenced earlier. If my wife didn't say something while riding with me, when she could clearly see that we were headed straight for an accident, she would have after the fact been saying, "I wish I would have said something." So, even if they don't consider or listen to what you have to say, at least you've put it out there and made sure that you're confident enough within yourself to make sure that you're always adding to any situation.

I've seen a lot of situations where leaders get into trouble or make major mistakes all because they only have "yes" men around them. They have passive people who are only along for the ride. When I analyze these situations, it's fairly obvious to me that what could have helped that leader was to have someone who could have grown with them, someone they could have trusted to say the tough things, such as, "Man, I know you want to have fun. I know that sounds good, but maybe that's not a good idea for us to go to this club tonight." Instead, as a point man, you could suggest something like: "Let's just invite some people over to the house instead of putting ourselves in harm's way."

Elaborating even more on the idea of a reliable person growing with the leader, it's always important to keep in mind that what you are trying to create is a team, and building teams is a process. The amount of time it takes to build a team and make it strong varies from person to person and group to group. It requires a certain degree of openness from both parties to facilitate the process. As a servant leader, you need to be open to the process just as you're expecting, desiring, and hoping your leader will be open to fully respecting you and receiving the insight you have to offer. Just as you want their expectations to be open, yours have to be open as well.

Sometimes, people attempt to take too much authority when they haven't built trust. You can't just expect the person in authority to just give you their trust. This is why the word "process" always needs to be at the forefront of your mind when you're first starting out and building your relationship as a team.

I can say team because that's actually what it is. Bishop Long and I are a team. We know our roles and the relationship is highly beneficial for both of us because we have mastered the art of being a highly effective team. I know and accept his strengths and weaknesses and he knows mine and values and appreciates what I bring to the table in the way of making his job and life much easier.

Another important consideration is that sometimes, it's not *what* you say to your leader, but *how* you say it that will influence the situation. You need to understand that there's an art to helping individuals, and leaders in particular, see the benefit in doing something they originally strongly opposed. You'll never win and be successful by simply trying to get your point across. The highest level of being an effective servant leader is having broad communication skills that are flexible and relative to the person you are communicating with.

A yes man knows that something needs to be done but will decide not to say it because they don't want to deal with the resistance or potential conflict. A point man, however, is willing to push through. They have much greater confidence because they've learned to develop and sharpen their communication and leadership skills such that they're able to engage in a process of dialogue that helps a leader—who initially had reservations and was resistant to their suggestion—shift their way of thinking and ultimately move in the direction that's best for the organization.

This type of ability to facilitate process, once again, is representative of the point guard analogy. Because being a point guard encompasses all the characteristics of a servant leader, it's a great way to visualize your role as a servant leader. The point guard, based on what they're observing and assessing about what's going on in the game, decides to make adjustments by calling a play. It, then, is up to the team to fulfill it.

Basically, in attempting to call a play, the point guard is saying we need to do something different and I have a suggestion for what we should consider. In that very moment, the point guard is also assessing how best to communicate what is needed to the coach, factoring in their personality and style of communication. While they are operating as an extension of the coach, ultimately, the final decision as to whether or not to run that play is going to be determined by the leader (the coach). When you become content and at peace with your role and value as a servant leader, you learn to live with (and not gripe about) the fact that the final decision is not yours to make. It's your job to ensure that you're doing all you can to positively influence the situation for the good of your leader with all the insight you have and can offer to yield a positive result. Know that you did your part and leave it up to others to do their part.

When you become content and at peace with your role and value as a servant leader, you learn to live with (and not gripe about) the fact that the final decision is not yours to make.

TAKEAWAYS

- A yes man just goes with the flow for the sake of avoiding conflict.
- A point man speaks up, always looking at the bigger picture.

- A point man has a great sense of timing for when to listen and when to speak up.
- Every leader needs a good point man.

Chapter 4

BE ON THE OFFENSIVE, NOT OFFENDED

"When you become a leader, you lose the right to think about yourself." — Pastor Gerald Brooks, Grace Outreach Center, Plano, Texas

THE ANALOGY OF SPORTS can be applied to so many life concepts. Just as we used the analogy of a point guard in the previous chapter, we once again here want to use the analogy of sports as it relates to having a mindset of "being on the offensive instead of being offended."

Just as the title states, there are two distinct approaches to being a servant leader that we want to address in this chapter. One is being offended. The other is being on the offensive.

A lot of times people don't make it to their destination that matches their life potential, or to finding the best role within their organization, because they become offended by the head leader. Or, it's because they become offended by other people saying certain things like, "You're just a do boy," "Can't you think for yourself?" or "You're a yes man."

When these types of things happen, you have to guard your heart and mind against being offended. You can't think about yourself. You have to keep your focus on what the ultimate goal is. You have to make sure you're able to do what needs to be done. That's precisely why the title of the chapter is worded, "Be on the Offensive, Not Offended."

I am a firm believer that as you truly dedicate yourself to making "it" happen for someone else that you will be on the journey you personally need to be on for your "IT" moment to occur (whatever that might be)! Your "IT" moment in my opinion happens when preparation meets opportunity. My father, who has been another great influencer in my life, would often make this statement to me in my teenage years. He would say, "Drew, when preparation meets opportunity, it breeds success. So, stay ready to keep from getting ready!"

These statements resound loudly in my inner man even today. They guided me to continually try my best to be offensively minded during my time of preparation until my "IT" moment appeared. So I can confidently say that if you can commit yourself to offensively and intently preparing yourself until your "IT" moment arrives, you will see the tremendous results it will yield in your life as a servant leader and as an overall person. Until then, while you are in your servant leadership role, you have to fully commit yourself to serving for your appointed time.

Now don't get me wrong. I'm not saying that the motivation for your serving should solely be with the mindset of: "I'm just doing this until I get my own." This is not at all what

I am saying. What I am saying is that whenever you find yourself with the opportunity to help someone else fulfill his or her dream, it yields many benefits for your own life. Many of these benefits can't be measured in the physical or material world. They have to do with your inner development.

Learning to be faithful in supporting and serving someone else is a major life lesson for all individuals learning to be effective servant leaders. Servant leaders have to be willing to sow into someone else's success in order to truly come into their own sustained success. They have to sow seeds and wait for their time of harvest.

Let me tell you this quick story about remaining intently focused and offensively minded in your service and preparation while on your journey. It begins with sharing a little bit about the makeup of my personality. Everyone who knows me or even sees me today recognizes that I am a very intense person when it comes to my physical fitness and the way I like to stay in shape. This was not always as easily seen. When I first started playing college football at Johnson C. Smith University in Charlotte, North Carolina, I weighed 145 pounds soaking wet. Even though I was a little guy in stature, I was absolutely huge in heart and effort. I am extremely confident that if you met any of my former teammates today, not one of them would disagree.

I will make this story short. When I got to college, I was what would be considered a late bloomer. I had talent. I was a pretty good receiver, but it just seemed as though I was always a few steps behind some of my teammates who were naturally thriving at the time. I was on a team with guys who just seemed to have the "IT" factor —guys like Craig and Desmond Brown, Jimmy Bell, and Derrick Johnson. They were just good players with immense talent.

While I would give tremendous effort, at the time, I just couldn't match up with their skill levels. What I did have going for me was a tremendous amount of discipline, focus, and perseverance. Where I lacked in natural skills at that time, I could not be matched or outdone in my effort or hard work to get better. While my aforementioned teammates thrived in games and were the stars of the team, I focused on being the best practice player I could be. I studied film religiously. I did extra conditioning on my own while no one was around. I committed myself to giving them as much as I could in practice so that they could prepare as well as possible for the games knowing that this would give our team a better chance of winning. You know what? It worked!

As I continued to help others get better and got them ready for the games, I became an unsung asset to the team during those seasons of preparation. I took pride in seeing them thrive in big game situations because I could confidently say that I had played a significant role in our team's success even though my name wasn't called. I kept this model of offensive preparation going throughout my freshman and sophomore years of college. I never got discouraged to the point that I lost focus on my goal. My goal was to help my team the best way I could and be ready when my name was called—at the moment where my preparation would meet the opportunity presented.

Fast forward to the first game of my junior year. As I continued to prepare myself over the past two years, opportunities for me to make more of an immediate impact presented themselves. My skills had developed. I was stronger, faster, and now weighed 189 pounds of muscle coming from the small frame of a 145 pound freshman. Amazingly, I had now become a starting wide receiver on the team. During the first quarter of my first game, I caught a 40 yard touchdown pass from Desmond Brown. It was the first touchdown of my college career. I went on to score three touchdowns in that game and was presented with the game ball from my head coach Tim Harkness. From that point on, I thrived as a college football player. I even went on to lead my team as the starting quarterback my senior year. The icing on the cake was being named the "Most Valuable Player" on our football team my final year.

This is not a fable or fairytale. The moral of this story is that I constantly stayed on the offensive during the years and process of my being in the background. When my number was called to take advantage of an opportunity, I was able to seize it. I was able to seize it because I didn't get bitter, upset, lose focus, or become offended when I wasn't put in the game. Rather, I prepared myself to be the best I could be within the role that I had at that time. The lessons that I learned during those seasons of preparation got me ready to thrive in my "IT" moments. Here are just a few examples of those valuable lessons I learned in my time of waiting:

1. Never get discouraged to the point of giving up!
2. There is always room for improvement while you're waiting.
3. Commit to growing while in the background so you can thrive when you're up front.
4. Find a way to make an impact from wherever you find yourself.

The above lessons are transferable to all walks of life and to all scenarios you might find yourself in while you're in a season or time of waiting. My story has a positive ending not because I was void of emotion; I did get discouraged. I was just mentally strong enough to never get discouraged to the point that I lost focus of my goal, which was to become a starter or to at least get significant playing time.

Many individuals become discouraged and allow their emotions to work against them rather than for them. They, then, fall victim to many of the dangers that come with being offended instead of being on the offensive. The greatest danger of all is that it blocks your vision. It's like walking around with blinders on or walking around in the dark. You can't see where you're going, which puts you and others around you in harm's way. Thus, it can cause you to sabotage those you assist.

Many individuals become discouraged and allow their emotions to work against them rather than for them. They, then, fall victim to many of the dangers that come with being offended instead of being on the offensive.

I easily could have gotten offended during my college football days and lost sight of the ultimate prize. I could have spent time and energy trying to point out the faults in the teammates in front of me on the depth chart. I, however, kept my focus, which enabled me to learn and grow (internally and physically) until my appointed time. I, thereby, was able to seize the moment.

This is just as true in whatever setting you find yourself, whether it be a role in ministry or a middle management role in corporate America. Individuals can't allow their personal egos to get in the way of accomplishing the overall mission. Men and women must take a long hard look in the mirror and ask themselves, "Are my interests greater than the interests of the team, or of the organization?" If the answer is "yes," then you are not operating with a mindset of service. It, then, may be best to move on to another profession or area of ministry that is not so dependent on strong teams working efficiently and effectively together to fulfill a major mission.

Every organization needs individuals who are willing to make sacrifices. Every organization needs team players who are willing to perform their roles and are content in those roles. They need people whose egos are in check to the point that it does not jeopardize the efforts of the entire team.

Getting offended doesn't do anyone any good. In fact, it hurts you and it hurts your organization. What I have found is that when I find myself feeling offended in my role as a servant leader, what's really happening is that I'm losing sight of the big picture. In these moments, I am starting to let my ego take precedence over what I know my calling and my function requires.

I might take offense if my boss told me that he didn't like the way I handled a situation with another co-worker or the results of a project I have presented. I could begin to pout, deflect, or try to make excuses about why things are the way they are. The thing is that none of those reactions add value to the situation. What am I gaining from this? What do I gain from presenting a rebuttal versus asking "What can I do better?" "How could this be improved?"

The overall theme here is that in order to have the ability to respond with this positive posture, you have to die to yourself. What I mean by die to yourself is best expressed in this biblical scripture:

> What actually took place is this: I tried keeping rules and working my head off to please God, and it didn't work. So I quit being a "law man" so that I could be God's man. Christ's life showed me how, and enabled me to do it. I identified myself completely with him.

> Indeed, I have been crucified with Christ. My ego is no longer central. It is no longer important that I appear righteous before you or have your good opinion, and I am no longer driven to impress God. Christ lives in me. The life you see me living is not "mine," but it is lived by faith in the Son of God, who loved me and gave himself for me. I am not going to go back on that. Is it not clear to you that to go back to that old rule-keeping, peer-pleasing religion would be an abandonment of everything personal and free in my relationship with God? — Galatians 2:19-20 (*The Message*)

In short, this scripture tells us that we have to crucify our own feelings, which includes feeling like we have something to prove to others. It also says that we are not to walk around allowing our egos to control how we respond.

This has helped me over the years when I am tempted or when I do get offended by criticism or discipline in times of servant leadership. When I get offended, I have to stop and ask myself: "Why are you upset? Why are you letting this get to you?" The answer that rings loudly each time is, "Because you're too alive." I have to come back to living in the principle of "A dead man can't feel offense."

Don't get me wrong. Walking and responding in this posture is not easily accomplished. It takes an intentional effort to operate this way and respond correctly in moments of trial. The key is to not allow offenses to overtake you and begin to harden your heart. This is important because if you harden your heart because you feel offended or have been offended, you will begin to see everything through a filter of hurt and attack. There is a saying that says, "The heart remembers more than the mind." In other words, many times we say that we have forgiven someone when we really haven't. You could try to think your way through situations, but if your heart is still holding on to negative emotions, then you won't be able to move forward in a healthy and effective way.

> If you harden your heart because you feel offended or have been offended, you will begin to see everything through a filter of hurt and attack.

What is the remedy for an individual who feels slighted and has a hardened heart? The answer is multi-layered. First, the individual needs wise council or someone they trust to help them see the harm they are causing to themselves and others. If the individual has a hardened heart and is not willing to be honest and work through their emotions, then you are limited in being able to help them. If they, however, are willing to own their feelings of anger and resentment, support can be offered to help them through the process of becoming more content with where they currently are in life.

MENTAL EXERCISE

Take a moment and reflect on some areas where you have hardened your heart. It may be with a leader, with a family member, your spouse, or an organization.

Whatever individuals you discover you have unresolved feelings of resentment toward, I urge you to release the offense so that you can move forward in your full potential of what's being prepared for you. It can only be seen and received by you when you are not looking through the lens of offense.

WHAT DOES IT MEAN TO BE ON THE OFFENSIVE?

Being on the offensive means constantly being in a state

of adding value to all those you're around. It is being a completer, being the answer, being a problem-solver. It is always making sure that stuff is getting done without complaining or seeking personal recognition.

Being on the offensive means always thinking ahead. As the point guard of the team, you have to anticipate what challenges lie ahead and position your team members to respond accordingly. This is what championship teams do. They do upfront work. They are constantly in a state of preparation, prioritizing and quickly responding to new scenarios that present themselves. Some tangible examples of this would be mapping out travel plans for your leader, going ahead of your leader to survey a venue where he's going to speak before his arrival, or maintaining and updating an extra set of critical items.

More broadly, churches need to survey and assess the needs of their community. They must ask some very tough questions and be prepared to follow through with a plan of action. How can our church make the most immediate impact in our community? What kinds of programs do we need to put in place to get kids off the street? What other programs do we need to put in place, and how can I as a servant leader assist my leader in developing and executing a plan of action?

Being on the offensive means that even when you have ideas you would like to propose, you never bring a suggestion to your leader without first carefully researching all angles and solutions to the problem. I never bring even a suggestion to Bishop Long without telling him, "These are the things that I have already looked at. These are the things that we possibly can do and how we can possibly do it." I don't just bring the concept out there and say, "Oh man that's terrible." My job is not to bring him problems.

It's to bring him problems with some type of solution or a chance for a solution.

We opened this chapter with the quote: "When you become a leader, you lose the right to think about yourself." That's the essence of service. It's giving of oneself for the benefit and blessing of others. To be able to serve, to have something of value to offer is a blessing, but you have to be able to see it that way. You have to be able to see the "big picture"—that everyone has a role to play. While the leader may get all the recognition because they're the one who's out in front, the truth of the matter is that none of it would be possible if you as the point person were not orchestrating things behind closed doors. That's where you have to find your glory. You have to find your call to fame in knowing that your role is invaluable to the overall success of the purpose, mission, and goal.

TAKEAWAYS

- Becoming offended can inhibit your progress.
- When you are on the offensive, you are always thinking ahead.
- Never bring a problem without bringing a solution.

Chapter 5

THE BURDEN AND THE BLESSING

"Steward your seconds because seconds turn into minutes, minutes turn into hours, and hours turn into days." — Andrew Momon, Jr.

IN THE PREVIOUS CHAPTER, we talked a lot about self-sacrifice. I can't stress this enough. When you are a servant leader, you literally commit your life to serving others for the benefit of a stated goal. That is your primary purpose in life. This is why I call it "a burden" and "a blessing." The burden is and can be the work and the output needed to accomplish the goal. The blessing becomes the benefits you get along the road or journey of accomplishing the goal as well as what you later receive when you finally accomplish the goal.

THE BURDEN

Tremendous responsibility comes with being a servant leader. You should understand this going in. Before making a commitment to a cause that requires your skills and where people will rely upon you, you should be fully aware of what is entailed. Not being the head leader, you lose some control of your schedule, your time, and your life for that matter. Your plans can change at a moment's notice. You may not be able to lead a normal life like the average person because you are not on your own time.

Serving others should not be looked at as a duty, but rather as a lifestyle.

Serving others should not be looked at as a duty, but rather as a lifestyle. This is especially true if you're fully dedicated and a really good support person. When you begin to embody this mindset, your leader will come to rely upon you. When their schedule changes, it means your schedule will change. When new priorities and/or emergencies are presented to your leader, it now becomes a priority and/or emergency for you.

Leaders heavily relying upon you also means that you will be entrusted with and privy to sensitive and confidential information. Subsequently, when you are a servant leader, in addition to your personal time being more limited and highly unpredictable, you also end up carrying a heavier burden of information than you would if you were only carrying your own responsibilities. The more confidential information you receive, the greater the responsibility. When you think about it, the very word "service" literally implies that you are carrying or facilitating something that is not truly yours or that you are a conduit for something to get from one destination to another. Inevitably, then, your role as a servant leader will require that a lot of weight be placed on your shoulders. You need to be prepared for that.

You need to count the costs before taking on more than you can handle.

The best analogy I can give you comes from one of my college experiences while enrolled in a business and economics course. I learned a term that has stuck with me all these years. The term is "opportunity cost," which can be defined as:

> A benefit, profit, or value of something that must be given up to acquire or achieve something else. Since every resource (land, money, time, etc.) can be put to alternative uses, every action, choice, or decision has an associated opportunity cost.
>
> Opportunity costs are fundamental costs in economics, and are used in computing cost benefit analysis of a project. Such costs, however, are not recorded in the account books but are recognized in decision making by computing the cash outlays and their resulting profit or loss.[1]

Let's say, for example, that a CEO has a major decision to make with regards to buying one of its competitors. Buying out the competition would clearly provide the company with a clear advantage by eliminating one of its competitors. However, the competitor's asking price falls far above the threshold of what the company's financial team had already determined would be a comfortable amount to spend without depleting the company's cash flow, cash reserves, and emergency savings. The dollar amount the competitor is asking for makes the deal too risky. In the end, the CEO decides the company cannot make the deal because the opportunity costs are too great. What will be gained does not

---

1. *http://www.businessdictionary.com/definition/opportunity-cost.html#ixzz3ZnUaYo57 (businessdictionary.com).*

outweigh what the company must give up in terms of cash, manpower, time, and energy.

The above definitions are technical breakdowns of the term opportunity cost. In a nutshell, it simply means that each moment you are giving up something in order to get or accomplish something else. Opportunity cost encompasses making decisions based on what is important to you while weighing and factoring what can be yielded by taking that particular course of action.

However, the comparison between how opportunity costs can be applied to the business world and how they can be applied to being a servant leader is not exactly the same. The difference is that businesses only focus on the bottom line—dollars and cents. Servant leaders, on the other hand, are not constantly factoring what immediate gratification can be gained in the "now" from giving up one's time and resources.

As a servant leader, you are constantly trading off moments for a result or a goal that is directly tied to the success of the team rather than one's personal gain. Oftentimes, people perceive this type of mentality as being outrageous or unattainable. It is seen as only for a special breed of people who don't have goals of their own and are only living life for other people. The truth of the matter, however, is that the servant leader who can exemplify this type of mindset is many times actually more focused, more determined, and more intent about their life path than someone who only wants to look at and focus solely on their own goals and dreams. A person who can show this type of selflessness is one who understands the power that lies within them as well as the influence they have to be an answer to a problem. They realize that they can trade off a moment of self-gratification in order to join forces with someone else—in order to accomplish a goal larger than themselves, one that has the potential of affecting and helping many times the amount of people they could have affected alone.

Furthermore, they realize that as they take on someone else's burden for the time being, they are not only sowing seeds of effort, energy, resources, and knowledge into another person's goals, they also have the opportunity to make tremendous personal gains in the process, gains that cannot easily be measured. They gain experience, and they grow as individuals.

Servant leadership can be a cyclical process that continues to feed itself. There are points in the cycle where we are givers and other points where we are receivers. Oftentimes, because servant leaders were willing to make a temporary sacrifice, they set themselves up to receive a great harvest of other servant leaders who embody the same attributes helping and sowing into their life vision the way they once did for someone else.

THE BLESSING AND BENEFITS OF SERVANT LEADERSHIP

I want to bring attention to two sides of the blessings that can be gained when operating in true servant leadership. They work hand-in-hand. One aspect of the blessing actually is what you're giving off or giving to others in the way of service and self-sacrifice. The other aspect is how you individually are blessed by having the opportunity to learn and grow while you're being a blessing to others. I'm a firm believer that when you commit to seeing the vision and dreams of someone else realized, you are sowing seeds for your own dreams to be accomplished. Ralph Waldo Emerson said it this way: "It is one of the beautiful compensations of life that no man can sincerely try to help another without helping himself."

While you are on the journey of life, you have a tremendous opportunity to learn invaluable lessons and reap benefits that you wouldn't have seen if you were not in the midst of the service opportunities that you partake in. This has certainly been true in my own personal life. I have traveled to many foreign countries, met extraordinary people—who are phenomenal leaders in their own right—and sat at the table of major decision-making and strategic planning sessions. The exposure and opportunities to sharpen my skills as an effective leader cannot be measured in dollars and cents or by the title I hold. My story, however, may not be the best example because not everyone who serves as a servant leader or assistant gets to travel or has some of the same perks with their job description. If that's the case, then you have to find the nuggets and kernels of reward that will hold you over until something more tangible appears.

You should keep at the forefront of your mind that in everything you do, in whatever role you are performing, there are opportunities for skill development. You must have cemented in your mind that you are a leader who is worthy of being entrusted with the same amount of responsibility as your head leader. Knowing that, you have to view the current moment as your test, your proving ground.

More than anything, it all comes back to possessing "The Right Psychology of a Servant Leader." This was expounded upon in Chapter 1. Your psychology, thinking, and view of your role is the foundation for everything else. If that's distorted, then you will be offended. You will view your role as a burden. You will see the glass as half empty rather than half full.

Once again, this book is intended to be a guide to effective and transformational leadership. In order to embody this, you must keep the heart and the mindset of serving others as the primary focus that drives you. So, you don't have to be a finished product. Own where you are and commit to the process of removing any internal barriers to sacrificing and serving others. If your heart is in the right place, you can learn over time to be an effective servant leader, and you will, without a shadow of a doubt, begin to see your influence become more effective and in time transform situations for the good.

TAKEAWAYS

- Serving is not a duty. It's a lifestyle.
- Opportunity costs means giving up something now to gain something later.
- When you are helping someone else, you are inevitably helping yourself.

Chapter 6:

5 KEY ATTRIBUTES OF AN EFFECTIVE SERVANT LEADER

"Authority is always built on service and sacrifice."
— James C. Hunter, author of The Servant

LEADERS ARE NOT CREATED OVERNIGHT. While an individual may be born with certain innate abilities, these abilities still have to be cultivated and shaped over time through various life experiences. Leadership, then, should be viewed as a process with various stages and an ongoing cycle of refining and sharpening one's skills, mindset, and beliefs.

The "5 Key Attributes of an Effective Servant Leader" chart below is an excellent tool for assessing your current strengths and weaknesses as a servant leader. However, before providing a summary of each of these attributes, I strongly recommend that you first take time to assess your strengths and weaknesses in each of these five areas.

LEADERSHIP SELF-ASSESSMENT "5 Key Attributes of an Effective Servant Leader"	
Self-Score (on a scale of 1 to 10) (10 = Excellent/Very Strong)(1 = Poor/Weak/Needs a Lot of Improvement)	
Attribute #1: Accept your role	
Attribute #2: Know how to anticipate the needs of your leader	
Attribute #3: Learn to master how one serves others	
Attribute #4: Listen effectively	
Attribute #5: Be quick to listen and slow to speak	

Now that you have completed a self-assessment of your current skill level in relation to each of the attributes, you should be better prepared to more immediately apply any new knowledge or personal awareness gained in your current role in service to others.

As mentioned earlier, many individuals do not have access to a clear path or process for cultivating the attributes of an effective servant leader. In this chapter, I will highlight five key attributes of an effective servant leader. These are attributes that I have cultivated in my own process of leadership development and likewise have helped others facilitate through workshops, seminars, and one-on-one mentorship.

ATTRIBUTE #1: ACCEPT YOUR ROLE.

"Leadership is best conceived not as a moment but as a cycle." — W. Edwards Deming

Accepting your role in synonymous with contentment. Otherwise, if you don't accept your role, you'll always be looking for something else to do or some other role to fill when there's already so much for you to do in your current role. Also, if you don't employ the mindset of contentment in service, you will not be able commit to developing the requisite skills that need to be cultivated before you are entrusted with leadership over others. I often have encountered individuals who—instead of getting all that they should out of the current place they are in—sabotage their futures by not stewarding their "now" moments.

My wife Dr. Momon often makes a statement that "we as servant leaders should stay hidden as long as we can because there will come a time when you can no longer hide and must take the front seat of leadership." What she means by this is that too often people try to accelerate to their time in the sun, or their time to be the frontline or primary leader, as opposed to enjoying the journey of learning. When you don't find contentment and fully embrace the current place or position you're in, you inevitably will spend more time trying to buck the system rather than learning to be a great follower yourself.

> We as servant leaders should stay hidden as long as we can because there will come a time when you can no longer hide and must take the front seat of leadership

In order to find contentment with where you are and the position you currently hold, you have to humble yourself. You have to find a way to serve with all you have as if the support position you are currently in is as high as you will climb; operate with such a standard of excellence within that current role that your attention is not distracted with being overly concerned about your personal career path or advancement. Rather, allow your mind to be consumed with exhausting every possible angle of your current function. This inevitably positions you for a progression of responsibility and influence should the opportunity arise.

Your motivation for this mindset shouldn't solely be to see how you can progress. Rather, serve to the highest level of excellence where you currently find yourself. If you maintain this focus, I am confident that you will see yourself reaping advancement in the proper time. You have to believe that your current servitude is only a training ground for greater responsibilities in the future. In other words, you first must be willing to die to yourself as a servant so that you can be born again as a leader and a great steward of what will be entrusted to you.

Some individuals never fully come to terms with the idea of being a servant leader. It's something they're doing, but their heart is not really into it. Projecting a faux persona, they operate in survival mode just to get through the days. Deep down, internally, they're really secretly wishing for and looking for their next advancement in rank and position. Therefore, they are never able to fully embrace a form of service in which their ego is removed and they find joy in being of service to others and being a completer of others.

Your desire should be to have the mantle of responsibility passed to you when it's time. Rushing your development and not valuing the process actually hurts you more than it helps you. By failing to be exposed to the right scope of things, you run a far greater risk of not fully developing as a leader with the right mindset and with the right skills because you did not allow yourself adequate time to fully mature. Instead of being guarded and protected during the natural process of leadership development and responsibility, your deficiencies will be exposed. While you may not be able to see it in the moment, there is tremendous insight to be gained by having the luxury of participating in the process of closely observing the intricacies of major decision-making while not yet having the full weight of the decisions placed directly upon you.

ATTRIBUTE #2: KNOW HOW TO ANTICIPATE THE NEEDS OF YOUR LEADER.

The golden rule of servant leadership is to "do unto others as you would have them do unto you" (Luke 6:31NKJV). You must place yourself in the shoes of your leader to envision what they need to more effectively and more efficiently perform their duties and fulfill the overall vision and mission for the organization. In doing so, one inevitably is compelled to ask a series of questions: "What can I do to enhance or add value to this situation?" "What are my leader's preferences, habits, needs, and thought patterns?"

John C. Maxwell, a well-respected expert in the area of leadership development, offers many great insights with regards to developing leaders. In his book *The 360-Degree Leader*, he highlights nine "Lead-Up Principles" that all servant leaders should aspire to develop. A 360-Degree Leader is someone who is able to lead from anywhere in the organization and does not let title or position within the organization inhibit their leadership influence:

> In order to develop the ability to be a 360-Degree Leader, people must learn to lead up with their

> leader, lead across with colleagues, and lead down with followers. Each of these skills draws on different principles. Leading up is the process of influencing a leader. The principles of leading up greatly increase the chance for success. Success in this case would mean leaders above will learn to trust and rely on subordinates in addition to seeking advice from them.

This type of trust only comes when the primary leader sees that the assistant or team member genuinely takes pride in their overall well-being. This trust that is built over time not only develops an opportunity for the servant leader to be more in tune with the leader, but it also positively influences them upwardly by seeing needs of the leader before they are asked or requested of them.

John C. Maxwell's "Lead-Up Principle #5" directly correlates to "Attribute #2: Knowing how to anticipate the needs of your leader." In particular, it places an emphasis on "investing in relationship chemistry" and challenges servant leaders to learn to value the importance of connecting with people. In everyday life, we must connect with our peers, those we lead, and those who lead us. The truth of the matter is that "people won't go along with you if they can't get along with you." This means you have to:

1. Be intentional about paying attention to who they are and what matters to them on an emotional level.
2. Know their priorities: what are the things/duties that they have to complete? The better you know this, the easier it will be to connect with them.
3. Catch your leader's enthusiasm; this creates a bond between you and your leader.
4. Support your leader's vision: be able to quote and communicate your leader's vision to others.

5. Connect with your leader's interests: professional and personal. You should be able to relate to their interests and life passions beyond their job.
6. Understand your leader's personality/style: be able to conform to their personality to better work with them.
7. Earn your leader's trust: relational currency. This allows you to have equity of trust. This gives room for the relation to weather problematic times and/or mistakes.
8. Learn to work with your leader's weaknesses: respect them and don't highlight them to others but learn to work to bring strength where your leader is weak.
9. Strive to earn the trust and honor of the family of your leader. Because you work so closely with your primary leader, it inevitably will indirectly affect the family. So, keep in mind, that they are an extension of the role he serves in.

ATTRIBUTE #3: LEARN TO MASTER HOW ONE SERVES OTHERS.

I love to use the analogy of a concierge. When you check into a hotel, a concierge is there to answer any questions you have, and if they don't know the answer, they take pride in finding the answer. This is the attitude you should have when it comes to serving others—particularly in your role as the completer or personal assistant to a senior leader. Vigilantly pay attention to who they are and what they like. Know their likes, dislikes, strengths, and weaknesses. Deliberately study them so that you eventually are able to anticipate their needs before they make any requests of you.

One of the things that brings me joy is being able to see a leader smile when their assistant or associate anticipates their needs before they even ask. For example, having served my leader for more than a decade, there are times that people stand bewildered by the fact that we can almost communicate without words. Based on the scenario and situation we're in, I can read his body language and know what he may soon ask for and as a result already be in motion with *the answer* before he even asks.

Referring back to the concierge concept, once you tell the concierge your objective, they may ask a few context questions before then coming back to you with a full list of options. Getting that type of service can't help but make you smile on the inside. It's a great feeling! This is only possible because the concierge tucks away their interests for the moment and puts themselves in your shoes. They intentionally started to think as if they were you: What would you like? What is most important to you in this moment?

A large key to learning how to serve others is to do what you can to make them feel special. This is what you should strive for when serving others. Make them feel as if they have their own personal concierge and that you will stop at nothing to make their goals and objectives come to pass. By committing to this approach, you are practicing the principle of sowing and reaping: When you make things happen for others, you are sowing the seed of your own future harvest.

ATTRIBUTE #4: LISTEN EFFECTIVELY.

When first reading or hearing this attribute, it might sound like it's something that can easily be accomplished. But, it's not. The art of "listening effectively" is multi-faceted. Effective listening is not just hearing what they're saying in the moment. It's hearing with an ear to complete what has not fully been said. It's digging below the surface and finding the deeper meaning, nuances and subtleties of their particular style of communication and thought processes.

There definitely is psychology behind the art of learning to listen effectively. Leaders don't always know what they need, especially in the moment that they're expressing an idea. Many leaders are visionaries. So, they see the big picture but not the critical minor details that attention must be given to. They won't necessarily think through: What are the actual next steps that should follow if their vision is going to come to pass? More often than not, leaders are expecting you to be able to take what they tell you and be able to fill in the gaps. This is called critical thinking:

> ... the process of actively and skillfully conceptualizing, applying, analyzing, synthesizing, and evaluating information to reach an answer or conclusion.[2]

In short, much of what it means to be an effective listener is "filling in the blanks." It's thinking with the end goal in mind and how you will get there. It is a perfect example of why you should not view being a completer or personal assistant as a totally subservient role. Being a completer and the answer requires you to already possess some level of leadership skills because you have to be able to take initiative. You have to be able to develop strategies and then execute those strategies.

Bishop Long, in the past, has told me he wants to do a conference for leaders and pastors. Because I had learned to listen effectively, when I heard him sharing his vision, I immediately went into a mode of think-

---

2. *http://en.wikipedia.org/wiki/Critical_thinking*

ing about the next steps. As a result, I would then come back to the Bishop and ask context questions. Some were simply to ensure that I had total clarity as to his vision; others were to paint a picture of different scenarios if we were to really move forward with the planning of the conference. Listening effectively empowers and equips you to be the answer!

ATTRIBUTE #5: BE QUICK TO LISTEN AND SLOW TO SPEAK. LEARN WHEN TO SPEAK AND HOW TO SPEAK.

This attribute is a culmination of all the other attributes. By cultivating attributes one through four, Attribute #5 will inherently be developed as well. By accepting one's role, by knowing how to anticipate the needs of your leader, by learning to master how one serves others, and by listening effectively, one is much more likely to be quick to listen and slow to speak.

Initially, in one's role as an answer or completer, it is common for an individual to experience this as one of the most challenging attributes to embody. Fortunately, in my own personal journey, this was not the most challenging attribute for me to learn to embody. I only at times experienced the temptation to want to speak out of turn. Because of my prior experiences as a servant leader, knowing proper settings in which to speak and when to listen had already been ingrained in my psyche. I was fortunate and very blessed to have had a wide range of experiences prepare me to be a servant leader. Participating in organizations such as the Boy Scouts, being mentored in church, the Junior ROTC in high school, and other leadership programs helped to cultivate and reinforce a mindset of servant leadership.

For most individuals, however, learning to embody this attribute can be very challenging because they are full of energy and ideas and want to express them. They also may feel a need to try and prove that they are worthy of the position or title they hold, especially in a day and time where patience is not overly praised or seen as a quality to value and embody . Rather, immediate gratification or recognition is sought after.

I strongly believe that over time an individual can learn to be more patient and to trust the process of gaining respect for the insight of others. Once developed, an individual can then comfortably sit in a room with persons of authority and know precisely when it is time to speak. This is true even during times when you clearly feel that you have something beneficial that you can add. You won't allow the fact that you can't speak freely drive you crazy. Even though you may have great ideas or insight to share, you'll come to understand and accept that just because you are thinking it or feeling it, it's not necessarily your place to say it.

Developing this kind of restraint is a very important process that many young leaders-in-training need to go through. It requires you to learn to be a fly on the wall and to be patient. In the meantime, until that door of opportunity opens, you have to find a way to keep your focus on learning as much as possible. You have to trust that, at some point, you will eventually be invited to share your input.

In the meantime, find a way to maintain a positive attitude and focus on continuing to develop your skills as a leader instead of sulking and developing resentment. Learn how to listen more effectively and over time gain the respect and trust of the higher up authority figures.

Eventually, when you least expect it, you will be called upon by the same authority figures and well-established leaders to give your input. "So, stay ready to keep from having to get ready!" You never know how being ready with the answer can shift an entire situation, organization, or even your life!

In sum, completing others is an underlying theme throughout this book. For one, as previously stated, we are greatly lacking many servant leaders who are willing to go through these steps or through this cycle in order to truly be equipped to provide direct assistance and support to primary leaders. Equally important to note, however, is that there are many individuals who have the heart and desire to be effective servant leaders but lack the skills and knowledge to do so. My goal in clearly outlining the previously discussed five attributes is to provide an individual at any level of growth and awareness with clear stages or skills that one can focus on developing in the process of learning how to be a highly effective servant leader. Even more, it will enable an individual to continually refine his or her skills in the ongoing life cycle of growing as a leader, as a person, and as a more effective servant.

There are many individuals who have the heart and desire to be effective servant leaders but lack the skills and knowledge to do so.

TAKEAWAYS

- Attribute #1: Accept your role.
- Attribute #2: Know how to anticipate the needs of your leader.
- Attribute #3: Learn to master how one serves others.

- Attribute #4: Listen effectively.
- Attribute #5: Be quick to listen and slow to speak. Learn when to speak and how to speak.

Chapter 7

THE POWER OF MENTORSHIP

"No individual reaches his or her full potential without the assistance of others." — Andrew Momon, Jr.

IT IS MY FIRM BELIEF AND conviction that everyone needs a mentor. While you may have accomplished a lot in your personal or professional life, we all, in one form or another, seek and gravitate toward knowledge and instruction that will aid us in any endeavor. Mentorship is multi-dimensional and comes in many forms. Reading this book, believe it or not, is a form of mentorship. Watching YouTube videos, attending lectures, and so on are all forms of mentorship.

On our journey to becoming the most effective servant leader possible, I believe mentorship is a very important piece. When done properly, it helps reveal blind spots. The mentor-mentee relationship brings out the best in the student as well as the teacher.

One of the most powerful mentor-mentee relationships I have ever experienced has been with Bishop Eddie Long serving as my mentor. Initially, I was solely a mentee in the relationship, but, over time, I was entrusted with the responsibility of mentoring other individuals, some from near and some from afar. This has included, on occasion, serving as a mentor to Bishop Long in particular areas where I have developed my skill set and have become much stronger. Thus, in turn, I am able to give him insight in areas where he may have blind spots just as he has done for me countless times in the past. And, I'm sure he will continue to do for me in the future.

Thus, I have experienced both sides of the coin. Because of this, I believe that I have gained and possessed some invaluable insight on this topic. Over the years, in my observations of numerous mentor-mentee relationships, I have identified a number of recurring themes and principles. The overall theme is that there is a mutual benefit for both parties whether what is gained is clearly identifiable or more so of intrinsic value. In my estimation, the first and most important principle of leadership is "The Law of Navigation."

THE LAW OF NAVIGATION

The Law of Navigation can easily be described as trusting that someone sees and knows more than you do. This is a leadership law that has been coined by one of my mentors, John Maxwell. He describes the Law of Navigation this way:

> Anyone can steer the ship, but it takes a leader to chart the course. Vision is defined as the ability to see the whole trip before leaving the dock. A leader will also see obstacles before others do. A leader sees more, sees farther, and sees before others.

> A navigator (leader) listens—he finds out about grassroots level reactions.
>
> Navigators balance optimism with realism. Preparation is the key to good navigation. It's not the size of the project, it's the size of the leader that counts.[3]

To convey this concept in even simpler terms, here are a few definitions of the word "navigation."

The Business Dictionary defines it as:

> The science of determining position, location, distance traveled, and course to a known destination.

It can also be defined as:

> The process or activity of accurately ascertaining one's position and planning and following a route.

What does all this mean? In the context of a mentor-mentee relationship, it means that you need to connect with someone who has the ability to see farther than you do at the place you currently are. We all have blind spots. So, it can be an added benefit to have someone such as a mentor who is able to guide you around areas that you can't see on your own.

In the context of a mentor-mentee relationship, it means that you need to connect with someone who has the ability to see farther than you do at the place you currently are.

The best analogy I can give is that of when you're driving. If your side mirrors aren't adjusted properly, there's a chance a car can pull up on the side of you, and you won't see it. You won't realize it's there because it'll be in your blind spot.

3. *21 Irrefutable Laws of Leadership*, by John Maxwell

Out of instinct or fear, you may turn your head to look through the rear view mirror; in that split second of taking your eyes off the road, you're putting everyone's life in danger. What I am suggesting is—rather than placing everyone's life in danger, learn to trust other passengers to give you feedback on the proximity of other cars. Because they have a different vantage point, they can tell you what's beyond your peripheral vision.

In this instance, when we are talking about navigating one's life, I would say it can be looked at as an inner compass that guides an individual to decision-making that is beneficial, rewarding, and in alignment with one's personal and professional goals. As it pertains to the Law of Navigation, the accumulated experiences a mentor possesses produce a certain degree of wisdom and knowledge that can be applied to various life situations. This is how added value can be given.

We all need to be able to have someone who can look beyond where we currently are and have been to guide us up and around common and uncommon pitfalls. Mentors, undoubtedly, have seen and experienced things that the mentee hasn't. This is critical to those who want to get the most out of their lives and reach their potential in life and as servant leaders. In other words, when we don't have a solid mentor in our lives, we are relying upon our experience and knowledge base to make decisions. We may be successful. We may not. The idea is that, with whatever amount of success we have achieved on our own, we can exponentially expand that if a solid mentor is added to our lives.

The Law of Navigation is one that also states there is a certain amount or kind of insight that each person can give to another person based upon their experiences. We, however, must have the willingness to yield to what we don't know.

We have to be willing to put our ego to the side or at least allow another strong ego to temporarily share the same space. For the relationship to work, there also are other variables such as timing, commitment, and a willingness to invest time and energy.

WHAT TO LOOK FOR IN A MENTOR?

Before moving forward with our discussion in this section, I first think it's best for you to ask yourself a couple of questions. First, think back to any time that you've had a mentor or someone you really looked up to. Why did you look up to them? What were some of the qualities they possessed?

I think that sharing a story with you of the kind of impact a great mentor can have on an individual's life will set the stage for you to gain even more out of our discussion in this section. As I've stated throughout this book, Bishop Eddie Long has been the most influential mentor of all the mentors I've had throughout my life. The fact that I've also been employed by him has greatly added to the opportunities for me to learn and grow from being around him. It also afforded him the opportunity to see me in a variety of settings that other mentors may not have been able to.

I could give many examples of the power of mentorship exhibited in our relationship. The most vivid example occurred eight years ago. It happened in Las Vegas, Nevada while we were eating at the Capital Grille. This restaurant serves as a memorial for me because of the significance of what took place there eight years ago. That moment literally changed my life.

For years, I had always prided myself on being a nice guy, and I was fully convinced that I was doing a great job in my role as Bishop Long's Personal Assistant. Bishop Long, however, had a totally different take on how well I was performing. One of the first things he told me was that I was very inefficient. The second startling comment he made on that day was that I needed to develop more of an edge. Too frequently, in critical situations, I was too passive.

His words were tough to hear, but for some reason, I didn't become defensive, in part because Bishop Long shared in a way that made it clear he wasn't trying to attack me. He genuinely was trying to paint a clear picture for me of areas that needed improvement. Subsequently, I took what he said and ran with it. I became a highly efficient person who was hungry for progress and very focused on what I wanted to get out of life.

Thinking back on that moment and the dramatic shift in my personality and approach to life since, I truly have been transformed into a whole new person. If he had not cared enough to be honest with me and had a willingness to push me past my comfort zone, this transformation may never have taken place.

Because I had given him permission to speak into my life, he was able to communicate the deficiencies and areas where improvement was needed. Also, because he was an effective communicator, it enabled me to be open and receptive to his criticism that day. I may never have been open to the same criticism from another person. Ultimately, that conversation shifted the entire trajectory of my life.

Now, having shared this story, which I think is an excellent story of the power of mentorship, I hope it will help you better understand and value the importance of a quality mentor in your life. There are times when I have to deal with new situations that involve factors I have not experienced. I call mentors for principles to guide me through it. Sometimes, just watching my mentor in action allows me to glean experience from them.

Some individuals are lucky enough to have the perfect mentor fall right in their lap. Others need to make a conscious effort to seek out and identify someone to serve as their mentor. Finding a mentor, however, doesn't have to be an anxiety-producing task. For starters, keep in mind that you don't necessarily have to have just one mentor. You can have multiple mentors for different aspects of your life. You, for example, might have a financial or professional mentor and then a spiritual mentor.

CHARACTERISTICS TO LOOK FOR IN A MENTOR

- Relevancy: someone who has qualities or accomplishments that you admire and aspire toward.
- Integrity: someone with good character whose walk matches their talk. Willingness: someone who wants to share their knowledge and expertise with you.
- Interest in you: someone who is willing to get to know you and your needs so they can best mentor you.
- Honesty: someone who will tell you where and how you could improve.
- Trustworthiness: someone with your best interests at heart, someone you can give permission to speak into your life.
- Shared values: someone with a similar world view, who knows what is important to you.
- Practicality: someone you can communicate with easily and often. A mentor on the other side of the world might not be the best choice.

- Availability: someone who has time for you. A willing and caring person who can't pencil you in cannot mentor you.
- Supportiveness: someone who will be there even when you fail, someone who will help you try again.

VALUING AND PROTECTING THE MENTOR/ MENTEE RELATIONSHIP

Once the mentor-mentee relationship begins, both parties must continue to be fully vested for the relationship to bear its intended fruit. Mentors not only must see potential in their students. They must believe in that potential.

The mentee has to value and protect the relationship of the mentor. Sometimes, when people find out who is mentoring you, they try to attach themselves to you with the sole purpose of getting to or having access to your mentor. You have to know that you then have become a door to your mentor. You have to be more aware of the significance of your role. You have to be more discerning in who you befriend.

It's a very critical key to understanding your role. So many times I see negative situations where people get in the door who shouldn't have gotten in the door. You don't have to block people maliciously, but you do have to filter them.

Mentees must believe that their mentor is the missing piece to them fulfilling their potential, while not taking for granted the need to continue to work hard and to push themselves. At the same time, just like some roles do not last forever, some mentor-relationships have a short span or run their course after a period of time or much sooner than we ever would have thought. Over the years, I've learned to more easily accept this reality. At all costs, I always strive to avoid any mentor-mentee relationship ending prematurely because of unresolved misunderstandings. Too many times, when that occurs, I've seen bad outcomes that ultimately are very detrimental to the growth and overall well-being of the student as well as the teacher.

What happens many times is that mentees fold under the pressure of accountability and the demands placed on them by their mentors. The mentees often start the journey well and then fall off after they feel that they know more than they think they know or that they're better prepared to take on greater responsibility than they really are. The tragedy is that they have fooled themselves into believing that they no longer need the accountability or the pressure that comes with it. So, they get off the bus before finishing the grand tour that was meant to fully equip them for their next destination in life.

> Mentees must believe that their mentor is the missing piece to them fulfilling their potential, while not taking for granted the need to continue to work hard and to push themselves.

TAKEAWAYS

- Everyone needs a mentor. Just as we're never too old to serve, we're never too old to learn from others.
- Invest in finding the right mentor for you.
- You're only able to get out of the mentor-mentee relationship what you put in.

Chapter 8

EXECUTING THE VISION

WORK SMARTER, NOT HARDER. Sounds simple, right? You'd be amazed by how many people—in all walks of life (including professional, educated people)—live their lives and conduct their business affairs in a highly inefficient manner. It is not always that they are incapable of efficiency and a higher level of productivity. They simply may need some refining.

Briefly referring back to the concept of a ground crew, which we discussed in Chapter 2: The Need and Value of Servant Leaders, I have already strongly conveyed to you the importance of teams. While often underutilized, so much more can be accomplished by working in effective teams rather than trying to do everything on your own. This is why, in this chapter, we are further emphasizing the importance of finding ways to work smarter, not harder.

Being a servant leader is filled with many trappings that cause men and women in service occupations to burn out, grow weary, and even sometimes develop bitterness toward those they assist. For example, the professional life span of individuals in service-oriented professions oftentimes differs drastically from non-service professions. Why is that, you might ask? I would venture to say that the number one reason is that so much has to be given of oneself to be really effective in a service profession.

Two examples of service professions that often have a short lifespan are doctors and pastors. This is according to an article in The *New York Times* (August 1, 2010). Doctors, lawyers, and clergy were reported to have the most problems with drug abuse, alcoholism, and suicide. Another staggering statistic is that approximately 1,500 pastors leave their ministries each month because of burnout or other areas of pressure.

The tendency is to feel as though one has to do everything, be everywhere, and know everything. That's just not true. It's also very unrealistic. Yet, many in the service industry feel and internalize this feeling of having to be superman or the savior, as if they can't ask for help.

Too many times, I have seen people burn out because they're trying to do too much themselves. Either they don't have the right team around them, or they fail to utilize them or delegate properly. Working smarter, not harder does not always mean that you have to be the source of energy that inspires and fills in the missing gaps for other people. It does mean making sure that you have the right people in the right areas to help you.

TEAMWORK MAKES THE DREAM WORK

You don't have to tie yourself down with things that you don't have to. If you really think about it, you could probably quickly come up with a list of things that could easily be delegated to someone else. This would include duties that you can break up for the team, like returning phone calls, filing paperwork, or running errands. Maybe you can find an intern to perform some of these duties so that you don't have to deal with them. It would definitely lighten your workload. That's the purpose of having a team, to make your life more efficient and to free up your time and the time of your primary leader to focus on tasks where your strengths are most needed. With that being said, I want to show a few examples that provide illustrations of how teamwork makes the dream work.

Greg Popovich: His basketball teams are known for the way they play as a team. It has often been said that the San Antonio Spurs are one of the most boring but winningest teams in recent NBA history. The reason being is that they work as a team to win. They accentuate each individual's strengths and what they have to offer in the context of what gives the team the best opportunity for success.

The story of 300: As the story goes, in 480 BC, Xerxes I, king of Persia, led an army variously estimated to be between 300,000 and 6 million men into Greece on a campaign of conquest. Realizing the threat, the Greeks, who were then organized into city states, sent 5,200 volunteers to the mountain pass at Thermopylae in an effort to slow down Xerxes' army and give the rest of the Greeks the chance to pull a combined army together to meet the onslaught. Led by 300 Spartans, the Greeks were able to halt the Persian advance for 7 days. Enormous casualties were sustained by the Persians as the disciplined Spartans, who, seeking to maximize enemy casualties, orchestrated a series of feint retreats followed by a quick turn back into formation. Coordinating this tactical maneuver—considering the chaos of battle—surely required extraordinary communication planning. We can easily imagine that other essential high performance team elements were present as well, including shared vision, operating out of one's comfort zone, being self-directed, involving everyone, and celebrating success.

Pyramids of Egypt: One of the original Seven Wonders of the World, the Great Pyramid of Giza, constructed around 2,650 BC, represents a clear example of sustained high performance teamwork by an estimated 100,000 workers over a span of 20 years. Composed of 2 million 1.5 ton blocks of limestone, carried 500 miles, the pyramid was originally 481 feet high with sides of 760 feet at its base. Begun and completed within the reign of the Pharaoh Khufu (approximately 2,589 BC to 2,566 BC), the pyramid was either intended as a monument to Khufu's reign or his burial chamber. In any event, there is little doubt that this massive team worked with a sense of urgency to complete the project as quickly as possible. Though probably designed by a single priest/engineer, the sheer scale and scope of the project strongly suggests a universally shared vision of the end result and wide-scale cooperation of planners in developing the methods to implement the vision and sustain the effort.[4]

All of these are examples of people doing things that would have been unattainable as individuals but more than possible when working as a team.

SMART PHONES ARE ESSENTIAL

Now that we have continued to build on the theme or concept of "teamwork makes the dream work," in this chapter, I also want to introduce you to some specific steps, tech-

---

4. See *http://highperformanceteams.org/hpt_history.htm* for more information.

niques, and tools that you can utilize to conduct your business affairs in a more efficient manner. These tips will help you to better organize your daily affairs.

The most essential tool begins with purchasing or owning a smartphone. I don't care if you're in the church or working in the corporate world. You can't operate in today's world without a smartphone. This is the center of your work-efficiency universe.

You receive and make phone calls on your smartphone. To remotely send and receive emails, you need a smartphone. It's a *necessity*. It makes life more organized and more efficient when you learn to use it properly.

You must have the right tools to be successful in working smarter, not harder. However, it's also important to remind you once again that "working smarter, not harder" is just as much a mindset as it is about having the right tools. It's a mindset of efficiency for you as well as your primary leader. You must at all times keep in mind that you are a personal concierge for your primary leader. You are a walking and talking rolodex of information. It's your job to know the specifics of what your leader likes. If he likes four ketchups, don't bring or allow someone else to bring him two.

You, for example, may need to research and see what restaurants have the best rating so that when you have to take a guest out, you can be certain to take them to the right place. You need to be able to quickly get recommendations and make relationships with restaurants for any city you travel to. When you come back to that city the next time, you should know the manager's name and they should know yours so that when you call it's like, "Okay, you're calling from so and so. We've got you taken care of. What time will you be here?"

By having a smartphone, you'll be able to record important notes such as these right in the moment. If you wait, you're bound to forget something important because something else will always come up unexpectedly when you are a servant leader. So, you must be prepared to record and then organize new information as it comes in. Your approach should always be to do it now!

The list of things you can record and store in your smartphone is endless. Here is a brief list of some common or important items:

- online research
- what's going on in a particular area
- events, entertainment, or hot topics
- expense reports
- packing checklists
- favorite restaurants lists

This list only touches the surface as to what can be recorded and stored for easy access. The main takeaway here is that there are many advantages to using technology to make your life easier. The most critical piece is a smartphone because its applications and how it can be utilized allow you to be extremely versatile in carrying out your duties and doing so in a highly efficient manner. So, be certain to purchase a smartphone if you don't already have one and begin experimenting with all the ways you can use it.

Moving on in this chapter, I'd now like to provide you with some additional tips—that are more practical in nature—for becoming more organized and more efficient in your role as a servant leader. These practical how-to's include how to effectively map your day and begin developing systems of operation designed to ease your load and give your arms the rest they need.

FOUR PRIMARY TOOLS NEEDED

1. Evernote

Evernote is an application that allows you to categorize and catalog different things based on different subjects. This provides for quick referencing, and it also allows for easy sharing of your stored data. More than anything, it allows you to think ahead and prepare yourself before unforeseen circumstances occur. I painfully know this to be true because I learned through trial and error. So, I now make it a point to always be prepared.

In the process of writing this book, Evernote saved me a lot of time and energy as I organized content for different chapters and different topics in the book. Here are some other examples of how I have used Evernote.

- Bishop Long
    - o I have a folder with the majority of the sermons he has preached. It includes where and when he preached the sermon as well as notes pertaining to each speaking engagement.
- Section for "Guest Speakers at Our Church"—I'm able to catalog what they talked about
    - o I may get on the road and be asked by the Bishop months down the road, "What did such and such preacher speak about?"
- Business things pertaining to myself and my business Momon Leadership such as:

  - o Corporation Filings
  - o Licenses
- A folder for personal documents

You can sync Evernote to your Mac, iPad, or smartphone. So, even if you don't have your phone or access to one of your devices, you can still access your stored data.

2. Calendars

Pertaining to calendars, my first recommendation is to create two separate calendars. One is for your personal agenda. The other is for your corporate agenda. Secondly, it's important that your calendar and agenda be linked and synced up with what your leader's priorities are. If not, you'll miss the boat and won't be as effective as you can be.

Personally, I use calendars in Microsoft Outlook in conjunction with Google Calendar. Whatever calendar you decide to use, make sure you sync it so that you can always access the information from the cloud wherever you are and on whatever device you are using.

3. Always carry a bag (Figuratively and specifically use a bag).

Good leadership does not just occur when you are present. It should be felt when you are not present. Everything should not fall apart when you're away. You should put systems in place so that the organization can still function and carry on properly in your absence.

If you have to take off for vacation or an emergency, while your leader is still working, you have to make sure your support staff has what they need to carry on. As stated earlier, I have a file folder that solely keeps all of the messages Bishop Long has ever preached. I have to the ability to share that access with my team members so they're able to function without missing a beat. Just by typing in keywords, any member of my team can access the sermons instantly.

More significantly, there's never a time that you see me where I'm not carrying a bag. This bag has become such an extension of me that I even go to the gym with one. It's all productivity related. It has my iPad, my phone, and so on. Because I work systematically, I can go in the dark with my hand and pull things out of my bag without directly looking at the bag. So, even when I'm not around, I can tell someone to go in my bag and pull out a highlighter or sticky pad. That's how well I know this bag, like the back of my hand.

Things that I carry in my bag are more for Bishop Long than for me. As servant leaders, we always put our leaders' interests in front of our own, because every primary leader has certain quirks or certain things that they need when they're in certain environments, and you want to be prepared to fulfill those needs. I accept, in my role as a servant leader, that it's not only my job to know what those quirks and needs are; it's also my job to make sure what my leader needs is readily available! Even when I'm not around, I need to make sure the needs of my leader are covered. In the end, that's what it's about. It's about supporting my leader and developing the other team members around him to provide what is needed. Study your leader. Then, continually anticipate their needs and be prepared to meet them.

4. Prioritization

In my experience, there are generally two types of people. People who make lists and people who try to do everything by memory. If you're one of those people who never makes lists, I doubt very seriously that you're retaining all the pertinent information that needs to be retained. Who knows? Maybe you have an exceptional or photographic memory and internal calendar as well.

Dates, facts, events, and priorities can become highly jumbled the busier your life becomes. As a servant leader, it is the norm to have tasks and duties dumped on your plate at the last minute. In just a few seconds, what you originally planned for your day or week can become unraveled. When curveballs come your way, it's much easier to set new priorities when you have a list of previous priorities to refer to.

Step number one is to get in the habit of creating and updating your major "To Do List" on a daily basis. Then, once you have an actual written or typed list in front of you, you can focus your attention on determining how to prioritize the list. Prioritization is making the most important things most important. In order to do that, you have to rank duties or tasks by levels of importance based on their role in you accomplishing your overall goal(s). Ask yourself: What are the most important things to get done or tasks to complete? What must get done today? What must get done this week? What must get done this month?

The goal is not just to execute the vision, but to execute the vision in the most efficient manner possible.

The ability to prioritize is a skill that can take time to develop. What's important for now is that you start practicing setting daily priorities and updating them throughout the day as needed. The goal is not just to execute the vision, but to execute the vision in the most efficient manner possible. In other words, you always want to strive to work smarter, not harder.

In this chapter, I have provided you with some specific tools, strategies, and techniques for organizing yourself and at the same time making life less stressful for your leader. Though this list of tools is not complete, I have listed—in my opinion—some of the ones that are most essential. These resources, if used properly and consistently, will help you tremendously in your role as a servant leader.

TAKEAWAYS

- Excellence = Commitment to Finishing
- Teamwork makes the dream work. Know that you don't have to do everything on your own.
- Prioritization is making the important things most important.
- A smartphone is an essential tool for maintaining organization.

Chapter 9

WHAT ABOUT ME?

IN THIS FINAL CHAPTER, there are two main objectives. Firstly, I want to reinforce the concepts that have been discussed throughout this book such that they become a part of your daily routine. Secondly, I want you to take a proactive approach to establishing and maintaining balance in your personal life.

Being a servant leader, particularly one who plays a significant role in the execution of the primary leader's vision and objectives, can be very draining. People are always tugging and pulling on you for your time and energy. Your schedule is jam-packed, and if you're married with children, you still have to find quality time for them. It can be a real juggling act.

I, therefore, feel this is a good time to provide you not only with some tools for maintaining balance in your personal life, but a head start on implementing a plan or strategy for maintaining balance. Before moving forward, I want to provide some context for what I want to discuss in this chapter.

On more than one occasion, I have had heart-to-heart conversations with personal friends or people I've mentored about work-life balance or ministry-personal life balance. These are people who are building teams, working with organizations, traveling extensively, and impacting lives all over the world. These individuals are high capacity leaders in their own right. They love helping people and love being the *answe*r to many people's problems. However, there is just one problem that often occurs as a common theme among my counterparts; they wake up one day and their wife is looking at them like, "What about home?" Or, if they are not careful, they wake up and realize that they have served everyone else well except for themselves or their families.

Many individuals who serve or are in support roles, much like those who are in lead roles, are very performance driven. We, at times, seem to get the most fulfillment in life from making things happen. We tend to feel most significant when we are taking people's calls, making sure that we are fixing problems for other people. You, however, can fix problems for other people all day long. But, if you're lacking in your own personal life and your own personal needs for yourself, what have you really gained?

The Bible says: "What does it profit a man to gain the whole world and lose his soul." I would venture to say, "What does it profit a man to serve the whole world and lose his home?" Think about that for a second.

The Bible says: "What does it profit a man to gain the whole world and lose his soul." I would venture to say, "What does it profit a man to serve the whole world and lose his home?" Think about that for a second.

What good is it to help everyone else make strides in life and to be all that they are supposed to be while you go home in shambles emotionally, spiritually, and even financially? Too many people fall prey to feeling they have to take on the savior mentality of fixing everything for everyone. Even though as servant leaders we are called to be *answers* to problems, we have to be careful not to live a life of imbalance, so I caution you to take heed and periodically take inventory of your personal affairs to ensure that any imbalances can be rectified before the damage becomes too severe to be repaired.

I'm not saying don't sacrifice at all or to stop helping people. What I'm saying is that, if you're going to maintain balance as a servant leader, you have to continually monitor your actions and your intent. You have to be deliberate and intentional in your efforts.

In my opinion, balance doesn't always mean you will weigh equally in the measures of giving and receiving or of personal sacrifice versus corporate wins. What being a balanced servant leader means is that you are in a constant state of self-reflection that allows you to both give your all and serve to your highest potential while ensuring you don't lose your stability in the process.

If you succumb to the trappings of imbalance in serving, you no longer are considered a blessing. You have now become the burden that you so intently committed to avoiding for yourself in your own life. You have become a part of the problem, not the *answer.* This is why I believe that, before making a long-term commitment as a servant leader, we must take a moment and take inventory of our motives. Why we are doing what we are doing, and what are our methods for doing so?

What happens when those people stop calling you to be the *answer*? Are you still content with yourself? Are you still happy being by yourself? Are you okay being alone, or do you always have to be doing something for someone else in order to feel fulfilled?

Serving and helping others is a noble calling, but you still have to make sure that you are healthy within yourself. Because, if you're not healthy within yourself, you're only going to be able to go so far. At some point, you're going to crash and burn. The wheels are going to fall off!

This is what I want to help you avoid. I want to help you begin now instilling a mindset that you don't have to be everything to everyone. As a leader, you can help develop others and put systems in place where you will be able to step away for a period of time and know that everything will be okay in your absence.

STAYING BALANCED FOR THE LONG HAUL

I have made my own mistakes. I have had to learn some very tough and painful lessons in this area. What matters most is that I did learn to take better care of myself and my relationships. I learned that, while I am committed to serving others with excellence, I have to have that same commitment to serving myself and my family with excellence. If you don't learn that lesson quickly, you will find that what started off as a calling and a noble commitment has become the archnemesis of the people who mean the most to you. Some of my experiences have revealed to me that I needed to make some major changes in my life in order to maintain balance. I began making those adjustments and continually do so in order to ensure that I'm able to be the best that I can be.

Setting time aside for your family is important. You, however, must also learn to set aside time for yourself. As servant leaders, we give so much of our time and energy to others that it's easy to lose sight or to get out of touch with our personal needs. This applies to our physical needs as well as our spiritual and emotional needs.

Before our behavior can change, our thinking has to change. We have to tell ourselves and learn to be comfortable with the idea that it's okay to think about ourselves. I think the analogy of picturing yourself as a bucket of water or as a water well is a good one to use. People are always coming to you and dipping from the bucket, from the water well. At some point, you will run out of water if you never refill. So, you have to make sure you refill yourself so that you can maintain balance and effectiveness.

It all begins with making a conscious effort to set aside time just for you. Even though I do a lot for other people, I use my personal time to engage in activities that build me back up. I might go to the gym and get an intense workout, practice ju-jitsu, read a book, take some time to go for a walk alone, or go to a sporting event. The most important thing is having that designated time where I'm not being the *answer* or the *completer* for anyone. This is my personal time where I turn off my phone and don't look at emails. I'm literally offline and inaccessible (unless in case of extreme emergency).

We all have a tolerance meter; we feel energized and positive for only so long. Then, once we hit that brick wall, our outlook is more pessimistic. We're more short-tempered. We're less tolerant. I have learned that periodically going offline is a proactive measure for maintaining balance. It ensures well-being for myself, and it also ensures that my family and those who work directly with me are not negatively affected by my behavior.

I have been serving and working in ministry for 14 years. In that time, I have seen a lot of people not have the kind of longevity they anticipated entering into their role or position. I have seen many people do well for two years and then quit. They become so burned out and frustrated that they no longer want to work in the church or even attend church. This happened because they didn't manage the cycle well. They didn't learn how to gauge their internal thermostat or recognize the warning signs of potential burnout.

My challenge to you is to make a commitment now for balance to be a long-term priority in your life. Don't underestimate how quickly you can lose control of your life. Without a plan in place and an understanding of the importance of starting now to develop the discipline necessary to maintain it, you are more susceptible than you think.

Step #1 is to begin with a self-assessment of where you are physically, mentally, emotionally, spiritually, and relationship-wise in your life right now.

- Where am I on this journey?
- Am I happy on this journey?
- What can I do to develop more balance?
- What are the things that I have to do versus things I just want to do?

Step #2 is to develop a written plan for maintaining balance in your personal life. An excellent starting point is to create "I will statements" in two key areas. You, then, can build from there.

PHYSICAL SELF

I will …

(Example: I will go to the gym at least two days a week for a minimum of one hour each day.)

RELATIONSHIPS

I will …

(Example: I will set aside at least one full day a month for my wife and kids to spend time together for a minimum of four hours with my phone turned off and without checking emails.)

Step #3 is accountability.

The power of mentorship was discussed in Chapter 7. In discussing maintaining balance in one's personal life, it's appropriate to reintroduce the concept here because it's applicable. A mentor can definitely provide accountability. However, many individuals may not have contact with their mentors as frequently as once a week or several days a week. So, you may need to consider someone else who is more accessible (a friend, a family member, a co-worker, or someone you see as a counterpart servant leader).

Once again, as stated at the beginning of the chapter, the goal here is to provide you with some tools for maintaining balance in your personal life. If you use these tools, you will greatly minimize the risk of burnout and of having failed relationships. Ultimately, the goal is to reach your full potential and become the most effective servant leader possible. This goal does not have to be accomplished at the expense of jeopardizing your physical health and your relationships with those you love. It requires practice and diligence to manage the juggling act, but it's possible.

In closing, I would like to present to you once again the Leadership Self-Assessment Scale (chart) that was initially presented in Chapter 6: The Five Attributes of an Effective Servant Leader. Take a moment to assess or reassess your strengths and weaknesses as a servant leader.

LEADERSHIP SELF-ASSESSMENT "5 Key Attributes of an Effective Servant Leader"	
Self-Score (on a scale of 1 to 10) (10 = Excellent/Very Strong) (1 = Poor/Weak/Needs a Lot of Improvement)	
	Score
Attribute #1: Accept your role	
Attribute #2: Know how to anticipate the needs of your leader	
Attribute #3: Learn to master how one serves others	
Attribute #4: Listen effectively	
Attribute #5: Be quick to listen and slow to speak	

As a teacher and mentor, my mindset is always operating from the perspective of: How do I ensure that my students are retaining what they have been taught? Even more, how do I ensure that what they have learned is being implemented into their daily lives?

With that being said, my hope is that as we're nearing the end of this book, you are feeling much more confident and have much greater clarity about how to approach your role as a servant leader. This is whether it's in a direct support role or on a voluntary basis. The Five Attributes are actual guideposts and measuring sticks for assessing the effectiveness of your skills as a servant leader. Further, the Five Attributes, and this book overall, are tools that can equip and empower you to be a *completer* and the *answer*. You can always refer back to them at any time to help you in your personal and professional journey.

The most important thing that you should always remember is to make sure that your heart and your motives are in the right place. Every day, approach being a servant leader with excitement and enthusiasm, even if you have not yet fully developed your skills as a servant leader. Just as leaders must be developed over time, even when they're gifted, the same is true of servant leaders.

There will always be problems and behind every problem there is a promise. Know that you have been created to be the *answer* to a problem. If you learn to see the problems and commit to being the *answer*, I guarantee you that beyond a shadow of a doubt you will receive the promises set aside for you!

TAKEAWAYS

- Stay balanced for the long haul. Being a servant leader is a marathon not a sprint.
- Make priorities in your personal life just as you do in your work life.
- Commit to consistently doing something that feeds you.
- Periodically assess your strengths and weaknesses as a servant leader.

ABOUT THE AUTHOR

Andrew L. Momon, Jr. is an expert in high-capacity, results-oriented, problem-solving leadership and service. He is highly sought after for his practical yet powerful perspective on leadership, life, and organizational structure and institutional legacy. Among his most important core values, he consistently seeks how he can add value to others. One of the ways he serves others is as a John C. Maxwell Certified Coach, Teacher, Trainer.

A graduate of Johnson C. Smith University, he led and served as the quarterback and captain of the football team while simultaneously earning honors as a four-time conference champion in tennis. Andrew served in these two extremely demanding athletic arenas while also spearheading and leading a weekly Bible study and prayer group through The Fellowship of Christian Athletes.

With more than a decade of experience leading and serving with one of the world's most sought out prophetic voices—Bishop Eddie L. Long—Andrew has traveled the globe as lead adjutant, special assistant and senior security to the Bishop. He also simultaneously provides leadership, direction, vision, support and results for several key ministry areas that he oversees in his capacity as Chief Ministry Officer of New Birth Missionary Baptist Church.

Andrew is a 2011 Executive Security VIP Security Service graduate and a 2012 and 2014 International Atlanta Open IBJJF Jiujutsu Gold Medalist. In his spare time he loves exploring all things new. Andrew and his wife, Kendra, reside in Atlanta.

CHAPTER 1: **NOTES**

CHAPTER 2: **NOTES**

CHAPTER 3: **NOTES**

CHAPTER 4: **NOTES**

CHAPTER 5: **NOTES**

CHAPTER 6: **NOTES**

CHAPTER 7: **NOTES**

CHAPTER 8: **NOTES**

CHAPTER 9: **NOTES**